Social Skills for Mental Health

Related Titles of Interest

Multicultural Assessment Perspectives for Professional Psychology
Richard H. Dana
ISBN: 0–205–14092–0

Suicide Risk: Assessment and Response Guidelines
William J. Fremouw, Maria de Perczel, and Thomas E. Ellis
Paper ISBN: 0–205–14327–X;   Cloth ISBN: 0–205–14328–8

Coping with Ethical Dilemmas in Psychotherapy
Martin Lakin
Paper ISBN: 0–205–14401–2   Cloth ISBN: 0–205–14402–0

Cognitive Therapy of Borderline Personality Disorder
Mary Ann Layden, Cory F. Newman, Arthur Freeman, and
Susan Byers Morse
Paper ISBN: 0205–14808–5   Cloth ISBN: 0–205–14807–07

The Clinician's Handbook, Third Edition
Robert G. Meyer
ISBN: 0–205–14230–3

Behavioral Family Intervention
Matthew R. Sanders and Mark R. Dadds
Paper ISBN: 0–205–14599–X   Cloth ISBN: 0–205–14600–7

**Handbook of Behavior Therapy and Pharmacotherapy for Children: A
Comparative Analysis**
Vincent B. Van Hasselt and Michel Hersen
ISBN: 0–205–13949–3

Health Psychology and Public Health: An Integrative Approach
Richard A. Winett, Abby C. King and David G. Altman
Paper ISBN: 0–205–14501–8

Social Skills for Mental Health

A Structured Learning Approach

Robert P. Sprafkin
VA Medical Center
Syracuse, NY

N. Jane Gershaw
VA Medical Center
Syracuse, NY

Arnold P. Goldstein
Syracuse University
Syracuse, NY

Allyn and Bacon
Boston • London • Toronto • Sydney • Tokyo • Singapore

Library of Congress Cataloging-in-Publication Data

Sprafkin, Robert P.
    Social skills for mental health: a structured learning approach /
Robert P. Sprafkin, N. Jane Gershaw, Arnold P. Goldstein.
        p. cm.
    Includes bibliographical references and index.
    ISBN 0-205-14841-7
    1. Social skills—Study and teaching.   2. Psychotherapy.
I. Gershaw, N. Jane   II. Goldstein, Arnold P.   III. Title.
    [DNLM: 1. Mental Disorders—rehabilitation.   2. Social Adjustment.
3. Social Behavior.   HM 251 S766s]
RC489. S63S67   1993
616.89' 14—dc20
DNLM/DLC
for Library of Congress   92-49061
                                                               CIP

Printed in the United States of America

10 9 8 7 6 5 4 3 2 1   97 96 95 94 93

For Barbara, Jim, and Susan

Contents

Preface

Approximately 15 years has passed since we published our first guide for teaching social skills to psychiatric patients. At that time our specific target population consisted of chronic mental patients who began to appear on the doorsteps of community mental health centers as the psychiatric deinstitutionalization movement took effect. Indeed, social skills training was in its infancy, with relatively few clinical applications: with chronic psychiatric patients, with unassertive and anxious individuals, and with a few preliminary efforts at helping people suffering from depression.

The intervening decade and a half has witnessed a number of interesting trends in mental health treatments. There has been a proliferation of psychotherapies and psychotherapeutic fads, many with a half-life of a year or two. Biological psychiatry, with its search for biological/biochemical/genetic roots of mental illness and its amelioration, has come into prominence among medical practitioners. It has been accompanied by an acknowledgement of and respect for empirical examination of therapeutic endeavors. In addition, a whole new lexicon has been applied to mental health service delivery, including such terms as "cost effectiveness," "accountability," "quality assurance," and the like, reflecting the impact of mushrooming (mental) health care costs.

As in years past, the mental health system has been called on to provide service to persons with an ever-expanding roster of social problems, including homelessness, AIDS, and drug and alcohol dependency. Needless to say, the increasing diversity of the patient population was not envisioned a decade or two ago. Despite these many changes in the mental health environment, social skills training has flourished, with empirically supported applications to an expanding range of presenting problems. In an atmosphere that demands more and more in the way of documentation, specificity of interventions, and efficiency, social skills training is receiving even broader utilization. For example, in recent years a number of psychiatric handbooks have appeared that review the recognized treatments for various psychiatric disorders. Social skills training is prominently presented. As an additional indication of the likely trend towards specification of treatments, a respected group of scientist-practitioners (American Association of Applied and Preventive Psychology) has proposed not only the credentialing of mental health professionals but the certification of psychological procedures as well. The demand for evidence of therapeutic effectiveness is clearly part of the agenda of cost-conscious insurance reimbursers.

Social skills training is no panacea. However, it is developing a very respectable track record and has the potential for meeting many of the requirements of the cost-effectiveness Zeitgeist without losing sight of its primary goal of helping people to learn and use much-needed social competencies to improve the quality of their lives. The present text is a guidebook for practitioners so they can learn to teach these essential skills.

BIOGRAPHICAL SKETCHES

Robert P. Sprafkin

Robert P. Sprafkin received his A.B. degree from Dartmouth College, his M.A. from Columbia University, and his Ph.D. from Ohio State University. He serves as Chief of the Day Treatment Center at the Department of Veterans Affairs Medical Center in Syracuse , New York, and is also Director of its Psychology Training Program. He holds academic rank as Adjunct Professor of Psychology at Syracuse University and Clinical Associate Professor of Psychiatry at the State University of New York Health Science Center. He maintains a private practice in Syracuse. Along with Drs. Goldstein and Gershaw, he has written extensively on social skills training with various populations.

N. Jane Gershaw

N. Jane Gershaw received her bachelors degree from Douglass College, Rutgers University, and her masters and doctoral degrees from Syracuse University. She currently serves as the Chief of the Mental Health Clinic at the Department of Veterans Affairs Medical Center in Syracuse, New York. She holds faculty appointments in the Psychology

Department at Syracuse University and the Psychiatry Department at the State University of New York Health Sciences Center. Her clinical work includes a long-term interest in therapeutic groups with various populations. Along with Drs. Goldstein and Sprafkin, she has authored a number of books on social skills training.

Arnold P. Goldstein

Arnold P. Goldstein, Ph.D., is the developer of three increasingly comprehensive approaches to prosocial skills training, *Skillstreaming* (Goldstein, 1980), *Aggression Replacement Training* (Goldstein & Glick, 1987), and *The Prepare Curriculum* (Goldstein, 1988). In doing so, his joint concern has been curriculum development and evaluation, as well as devising instructional techniques for the purpose of effective trainer training. His development, evaluation, and training efforts have focused primarily on enhancing the prosocial skills proficiency of aggressive adolescents and younger children in school and agency settings. Reflecting his role as Director of the Syracuse University Center for Research on Aggression, much of his research and teaching have centered on helping youngsters replace antisocial, aggressive behaviors with constructive, alternative means of seeking life satisfaction and effectiveness. Because his early evaluation research increasingly indicated that most youth do learn, but fail to transfer or maintain such newly learned prosocial skills proficiency, his research came more and more to focus on the development and evaluation of diverse procedures for increasing the likelihood that such setting and temporal generalization would in fact become more likely to occur—a major research interest of his which continues.

Professor Goldstein is also author or editor of such books as *Therapist-Patient Expectancies in Psychotherapy, Psychotherapeutic Attraction, The Lonely Teacher, Youth Violence, School Violence, Aggression in Global Perspective, In Response to Aggression, Delinquents on Delinquency, Delinquent Gangs: A Psychological Perspective,* and *The Gang Intervention Handbook.*

He is currently Professor of Special Education, Syracuse University. Professor Goldstein was the recipient of the 1990 Award Excellence from the Juvenile Justice Training Association and the 1991 Donald G. Blackburn Award from the National Association of Juvenile Correction Agencies. He is co-director of the New York State Task Force on Juvenile Gangs and a member of the American Psychological Association Commission on Youth Violence.

Chapter 1

Introduction: The Skill-Deficient Client

A century and a half ago, treatment of the chronically mentally ill was undergoing great changes. The following statement appeared in the *American Journal of Insanity:*

> The removal of the insane from home and former associations, with respectful and kind treatment under all circumstances, and in most cases manual labor, attendance on religious worship on Sunday, the establishment of regular habits and of self-control, diversions of the mind from morbid trains of thought, are now generally considered as essential in the Moral Treatment of the Insane.(*American Journal of Insanity*, 1847, p.1)

Just as the mid-nineteenth century brought great optimism for the treatment of the chronically mentally ill, so too did such optimism reemerge a little over a century later. But, instead of viewing the psychiatric institution as the solution, mid-twentieth century mental health professionals and policy makers saw it as the problem. The fervor to move psychiatric patients out of institutions paralleled the impetus for movement in the opposite direction that occurred one hundred years earlier. Indeed, with over 550,000 psychiatric inpatients spending an average of 6 months during each hospitalization in 1955, the public was ripe for a less costly alternative. Moreover, the shortcomings and abuses of psychiatric institutions stirred the consciences of many. As a catalyst, the introduction of major tranquilizers provided the means for moving large numbers of chronic, institutionalized, "colonized" inpatients into the community where they could reenter the mainstream of society. The continued treatment that would be necessary for the newly deinstitutionalized patients would take place in community mental health centers, established largely under the auspices of the 1963 Community Mental Health Centers (CMHC) Program (P.L. 88–164).

1

These newly deinstitutionalized mental patients, most of whom were diagnosed as schizophrenic, were generally ill-equipped to meet the challenges they encountered when entering society outside of the walls of the psychiatric institutions. These people have been characterized as "skill-deficient"—lacking those skills or competencies necessary to survive adequately in mainstream society. Such persons were often unemployed, living in single-room occupancies or homeless, unable to avail themselves of medical care, and lacking the social skills to deal effectively with their interpersonal environments. The treatment facilities entrusted with the responsibility for providing care for these patients were often not prepared to do so. Medication alone was not the panacea. Although antipsychotic drugs helped control hallucinations and delusions, the so-called positive symptoms of schizophrenia, these drugs had little impact on the negative symptoms, such as apathy and withdrawal (Bellack, 1989). Nor did these medications supply the skills necessary to survive outside of the institution (Diamond, 1985; Goldstein, Sprafkin, & Gershaw, 1976).

> The year was 1969. Blanche was 55 years old. She had been living in a ward of a state psychiatric center for the past 30 years. Although early records were sketchy, Blanche originally came into the psychiatric hospital because she was penniless, ill-clothed, and found wandering around the streets of Chicago with no place to go. The hospital provided her with her basic needs, and soon Blanche became a model patient. She frequently did chores for staff such as ironing and general housekeeping. She was compliant with hospital routines and settled in for a long stay.
>
> When the community mental health movement finally made its way into Blanche's ward, the community placement team was faced with a woman who was nonpsychotic, pleasant, polite, and willing to do all kinds of work for little or no money. She had no idea how to take a bus, cook a meal, or read a telephone book. Although she had many social skills that were appropriate for hospital living, she had few of the assertiveness skills needed to survive outside of the institution. Whereas compliance was the route to survival in the hospital, it was certainly not going to help her out on the street.

Most mental health professionals working in community mental health centers were best prepared to provide verbal psychotherapy, but verbal psychotherapy was not usually the primary need of chronic psychiatric patients who were referred to them for services. What these persons needed was food, clothing, shelter, money, social skills training, medical assistance, sheltered employment, social services, crisis management, and the like, but community mental health centers were not financially able or conceptually ready to deliver so wide a range of services. It is no wonder that many community mental health centers, in attempting to do what they did well, i.e., verbal psychotherapy, began to attract new kinds of clients who were glad to be able to receive otherwise costly mental health services at low fees. These were not the clients who were envisioned originally as populating community clinics supported largely by public funds, but they clearly were good psychotherapy candidates. These "worried well" clients appeared as embodiments of the ideal recipient of psychotherapy, Mr. YAVIS—Young, Attractive, Verbal, Intelligent, Successful—whom William Schofield (1964) first introduced a generation ago. Providing psychological treatment/psychotherapy for YAVIS clients did not create conceptual difficulties for community mental health center staff. These unanticipated but "treatable" clients were anxious, were mildly to moderately depressed, experienced adjustment problems, and responded well to a variety of psychotherapies. Only their numbers on the caseloads of community mental health centers caused difficulties. Rather, providing appropriate psychological treatments for the other applicants referred to the CMHCs is what caused the dilemmas.

Not all of the problematic applicants for services were deinstitutionalized psychiatric patients. In fact, a whole new group of difficult-to-treat, skill-deficient patients were directed to community-based clinics. These were the never institutionalized people in their twenties or thirties who were now seeking services from the community mental health system. These "young chronics" also were often diagnosed as schizophrenic, but without years of institutionalization.

> Arthur was 35 years old. He had always lived with his parents. He had never set foot inside a community mental health center until he was 33. Until then, his parents had managed to shelter him from the system by putting up with his odd behaviors, his hallucinations, and his childlike inability to function independently.
>
> Arthur was the last in a long line of children. He had been labeled "emotionally disturbed" from an early age and had been in special education classes most of his school years. Because of his strong family connections, he never required inpatient hospitalization. Because of his parents, grandparents, and older siblings, he was able to live in the community, even during periods when he was actively psychotic.
>
> When Arthur stopped agreeing to attend school, his parents let him stay at home. The school psychologist strongly advised them to enroll Arthur in a sheltered workshop or a day treatment program, but Arthur's parents saw no need to do so. After all, they were healthy, Arthur was company for his mother during the day, and they found his behavior to be less of a problem once social workers and psychologists stopped meddling in family business.
>
> When Arthur's mother had a stroke and required nursing home placement, the family's problems with Arthur, the adult, began. With no one to supervise him during the day, he was often found wandering the streets. On several occasions he was brought home by the police after being picked up for shouting in public buildings and once for walking into a women's

restroom. Arthur's family had no choice but to enter the community mental health system.

On intake evaluation, Arthur was diagnosed chronic schizophrenic. He was socially quite skill-deficient, had some rudimentary self-care skills, and showed little motivation to do anything but sit and watch television. He was referred to a day-care program that eventually taught him basic social and prevocational skills. Following his mother's death, Arthur moved into a group home and worked in a sheltered workshop.

Others also sifted through various cracks to end up on the doorsteps of community mental health centers. Although many had similar needs and skill deficiencies as chronic deinstitutionalized schizophrenics, their treatment careers and diagnoses were different. Some mentally retarded individuals, particularly if they also carried psychiatric diagnoses, found their way into the mental health system. Likewise, others with dual diagnoses, such as MICA patients (mentally ill chemical abusers) were also sent to challenge the therapeutic talents of CMHC staff. Individuals with serious personality disorders, as well as those with cognitive deficits which might or might not be associated with brain damage (cf. Erickson & Burton, 1986), further complicated the treatment picture.

By 1977, the number of chronic psychiatric patients remaining 1 year or longer as inpatients in mental hospitals was 150,000, a huge decrease from two decades previous. The largest number of the estimated 1.7 to 2.4 million chronically mentally ill individuals in the United States were living in the community and relying primarily on community mental health centers for their therapeutic services. The rest found their ways into other support and treatment systems: prisons, psychiatric wards in general hospitals, nursing homes, as well as psychiatric hospitals. For example, it was estimated that approximately 750,000 chronic mental patients resided in nursing homes in 1977. Trends such as these led many to abandon the term "deinstitutionalization," with its initially optimistic connotations, to the more accurate, more pessimistic label of "transinstitutionalization." The shutting down of the asylum did not make the problem go away, but rather it created new sets of challenges for public policy makers and mental health professionals.

One could say that Mary grew up in institutions. She is now 22 years old. Her first foster home placement occurred when she was 1 month old and removed from her mother's care due to neglect. She spent her first 10 years in a series of foster care placements, during which time she exhibited a variety of problematic behaviors. She was self-destructive, often pulling her hair out or banging her head against walls and furniture. She was slow to learn in school and had already been held back two grades by her tenth birthday. It was in the third grade that a teacher noticed bruises on Mary's arms and legs. She had come to school particularly disheveled on that day and had spent the day rocking and talking to herself, paying little attention to the lesson. It was another child's birthday, and Mary hardly noticed the birthday cake that was being given to her.

The teacher sent Mary to the school nurse, who found more bruises on Mary. She also found Mary to be particularly uncommunicative. An investigation turned up the fact that someone in the foster home had beaten Mary. She was removed from the home and placed in the children's ward of a psychiatric center.

Mary's problems went from bad to worse. She began a series of hospitalizations, interspersed with attempts at foster placement. She was already excluded from the mainstream in school, attending a school for emotionally disturbed and other labeled children. Mary became more and more withdrawn and harder to reach. By her twenty-first birthday, she had spent approximately 8 years in hospitals and other residential care settings. As a young adult, Mary was passive, compliant, fearful, and withdrawn. She had been given many diagnoses through the years, including autism, mental retardation, childhood schizophrenia, and chronic schizophrenia. Regardless of the diagnoses, she was a woman who was unable to make even her most basic needs known to treatment personnel. With the opening of a group home for younger psychiatric patients in the community, Mary moved into a setting that would prove to be home for a long time to come.

This setting taught Mary many skills that had never been learned in years of institutionalization. She learned such concrete skills as washing her own clothes and shopping in a supermarket. She learned how to take a bus to the day-care program several miles away. She also learned a whole array of social skills, such as starting a conversation, asking for help, and making a complaint.

The immediate task of providing appropriate psychotherapeutic treatments to those in need of such services presents itself as a day-to-day issue for community mental health center staff. Added to the burden of having to develop appropriate therapeutic modalities is the further requirement of documenting treatment efforts and justifying the suitability and cost-effectiveness of staff involvements with patients. Indeed, a whole new vocabulary has emerged in mental health care, with such terms as "quality assurance," "DRGs" (diagnostic related groups), and "accountability" being heard far more frequently than the "id," "ego," and "superego" of past years. The stark reality of mental health treatment is, like all health care, exceedingly expensive to provide so that the expenditure of the public or private funds necessary to pay for such treatment is scrutinized very closely. Policy makers and mental health administrators must be as concerned with the "bottom line" as with the therapeutic needs of those utilizing the mental health system—if the system is not cost-effective it will not survive, and such cost-effectiveness must be demonstrable.

The day-care program of a state hospital had been a drop-in center for many years; probably it was started back in the 1960s. The activities included regular card games, assorted industrial arts and occupational therapy projects, parties, and the like. The patient population was aging and used to the routine and the loose structure.

When the new head of the mental health department looked over the records, she found a striking absence of therapeutic progress. In discussing the issue with staff, the response was always the same, "What do you expect from a bunch of chronic patients?"

The department head knew this attitude well and also knew that these progress notes would not pass inspection by the state team coming through in less than a year. There needed to be some documentation of problem areas in the patient population and some therapeutic work toward improving those areas. In looking at the passive, minimally communicative patients, it was clear that a social skills training program would meet both needs. Patients could be assessed for various social skill deficiencies, placed in groups according to their needs, and trained in a variety of skills. This behavioral approach was easily documentable. Furthermore, existing staff could be trained in social skills training techniques. No additional resources would be necessary.

Although the department head's approach seemed a bit too focused on the bottom line, and seemed to be unrelated to the needs and routines of the patients, the final product was hardly just "something administration dreamed up." Patients who were part of the program began to show some real improvement in their social skills, and, most surprisingly, staff enjoyed the new groups because they provided a break in routines that had gotten quite old.

At the same time as chronic psychiatric patients were being deinstitutionalized (or transinstitutionalized), a whole new approach to the treatment of many of the problems presented by such patients was in the process of development and implementation. Indeed, much of this development and implementation came about in response to the unique needs of newly deinstitutionalized mental patients (Goldstein et al., 1976). This approach has come to be called the *social skills training movement*. Merely moving patients out of institutions into the community was not sufficient to enable them to function independently, even with the use of antipsychotic medications. Most were deficient in the fundamental skills or competencies necessary for independent living.

Basic among these skills are social and interpersonal skills that permit one to negotiate one's way in the world. As suggested by Donahoe and Driesenga (1988), the theory underlying much of the social skills training work with chronic psychiatric patients has been referred to as the "vulnerability-stress" model, as presented by Zubin and Spring (1977) and others (cf. Bellack, 1989; Nuechterlein & Dawson, 1984). This model states that some people are predisposed genetically to develop schizophrenia. If their biological vulnerability threshold is exceeded by psychosocial stressors, they are likely to develop symptoms. Social skills training has been presented as an effective strategy for helping these vulnerable, at-risk individuals deal with some of the stressors in their interpersonal environments. Liberman, Falloon, and Aitchison (1984) suggested that social skills training can help the skill-deficient individual suffering from schizophrenia deal with two types of functions necessary for survival: instrumental and social-emotional. Instrumental contacts enable the person to meet basic needs (food, clothing, shelter, etc.). Social-emotional contacts provide a sense of belonging, well-being, and friendship. Persons with schizophrenia are likely to be deficient in the skills necessary to handle both types of interpersonal stressors. Improvement in social functioning, as facilitated by social skills training, helps reduce the vulnerability of these at-risk individuals.

Social skills training with chronic psychiatric patients is at least 2 decades old. When used with chronic psychiatric patients, it has gone by such names as "Structured Learning Therapy" (Goldstein et. al., 1976) and "Personal Effectiveness Training" (Liberman, King, and DeRisi, 1975), or more generically as "assertiveness training" or just "social skills training." It has frequently been combined with other treatments, particularly psychotropic medications. Often it has been implemented within the context of a day-treatment setting or other similar psychosocial rehabilitation programs, both inpatient and outpatient. One of the major conceptualizations of the treatment needs of chronic psychiatric patients is known as "Psychiatric Rehabilitation" (Anthony & Nemec, 1984). Borrowing from the vocabulary of physical rehabilitation, with its emphasis on enhancing the person's skills and abilities to cope effectively with his or her environment, it draws a contrast with the medical model's traditional emphasis on effecting a "cure." Among the skills to be taught within the Psychiatric Rehabilitation approach are social skills.

So ubiquitous has social skills training become that it has been discussed as a standard therapy with chronic mental patients in various psychiatric handbooks which review the range of contemporary psychiatric treatments (cf. Bellack, 1989; Borus, 1989; Karasu, 1989; Liberman & Foy, 1983; Kaplan & Sadock, 1989). Although there is still no totally effective treatment program for chronic psychiatric patients, evidence for gains made using various social skills training approaches has been persuasive. In reviewing approximately 15 years of empirical research on the effectiveness of social skills training with chronic mental patients, Donahoe and Driesenga (1988) found that patients were able to learn various social skills and to demonstrate their use in some naturalistic settings. Most such studies found evidence of skill use in training or clinic settings, with generalization across time and place proving to be more difficult, but not impossible.

Various approaches to social skills training share common components. Most can trace their common heritage to both education, with its emphasis on didactic teaching, and academic psychology, with its long involvement in the study of learning (Sprafkin, 1984). This latter path is also usually drawn through behaviorism and the behavior modification movement. Both of these traditions generally view behavior as largely learned; hence, it can be taught. Social skills are considered to be specific behaviors that may not be present or used frequently or effectively enough.

As is evident from the previous discussion, social skills training, although endorsed in recent years by members of the psychiatric community as an important treatment for chronic psychiatric patients, is not a product of mainstream psychiatric tradition. It is more compatible with the vocabulary of "rehabilitation" rather than "cure." It generally employs the terminology of "skill deficits" instead of diagnoses. Despite its eschewal of psychiatric diagnostic labels within its methodology, social skills training is most often used with persons who have been diagnosed with those labels. Its use with schizophrenics has been described previously. When used with persons diagnosed or described as "depressed," for example, social skills training is viewed as a remedy for persons who are considered to receive insufficient positive reinforcement in their interpersonal lives (cf. Becker, Heimberg, & Bellack, 1987). Either they have never learned the requisite interpersonal behaviors to elicit positive reinforcement, or they have too few opportunities to practice these behaviors, or they fail to use them appropriately. As a result, such persons emit fewer and fewer positive behaviors that are likely to be reinforced and, hence, become depressed (cf. Lewinsohn, 1975). By learning, relearning, and/or practicing appropriate social skills, these depressed individuals are likely to display behaviors that allow for "response-contingent positive reinforcement"—engaging in those interpersonal activities that are conducive to regaining a sense of self-worth, competence, and affirmation from others. Receiving positive reinforcement, in turn, is likely to lead to a decrease in depressive feelings. Depression, within a social skills training framework, is less of a concern as strictly a diagnostic issue and more of a concern in terms of the interpersonal skill deficiencies of persons so described. Indeed, the depressive feelings of these individuals may be due largely to these skill deficiencies.

Keisha married Lonnie when she was 16 years old and 7 months pregnant. She was a quiet teenager who never went out on dates or had friends. When Lonnie showed some interest in her, she passively went along. By the time she was 25, Keisha had two children, was divorced, and was living on welfare. A social worker at her child's school noticed that Keisha looked depressed and recommended that she seek help at the county mental health clinic. On intake, Keisha was described as chronically depressed. She had little to say about her problems, stating that she had felt depressed for as long as she could remember. She offered little in the way of elaborated answers to the intake worker's questions. She seemed nervous around people, stating that she spent most of her days alone in her apartment.

Among the treatment offerings at the clinic was a social skills training group. Keisha was enrolled in the group, as it was felt that she needed practice interacting with other people. Her social skills repertoire was lacking in even basic conversational components. Structured experience in such a group eventually helped to prepare Keisha for involvement in a single-parent support group. With a repertoire of social skills, Keisha's social isolation diminished considerably. She reported feeling happier and more capable of handling day-to-day social encounters.

One of the first manifestations of social skills training with persons described as anxious or neurotic was known as "assertiveness training." Dating from the work of Salter (1949), Wolpe (1958), and Wolpe and Lazarus (1966), these writers, and others, believed that learned responses of anxiety (often defined physiologically) interfered with a person's ability to express basic feelings and emotions and to stand up for one's rights in interpersonal situations. Such people frequently avoid potentially stressful interpersonal contacts because they have learned that avoidance, although not getting them what they wish or deserve, at least is momentarily successful in enabling them to avoid the discomforting feelings of anxiety. Thus, their anxiety inhibits the appropriate interpersonal behavior, usually at a price. That is, the consequence of this type of inhibited performance is that the person does not achieve his or her goals and also usually remains feeling dissatisfied or resentful. The objective of treatment within this framework is to overcome and override the neurotic habits (anxiety responses) so that the person's effective interpersonal behaviors can emerge. The techniques for accomplishing this goal have been referred to as assertiveness training and are essentially the same as the more general social skills training approaches. It should be noted that these earlier writers assumed that the requisite interpersonal skills were already part of the person's behavioral repertoire. What needed to be done therapeutically was to remove the roadblocks (anxiety) so that the effective, assertive interpersonal behavior could emerge. Later writers dealing with similar issues of assertiveness were less certain the person already possessed the relevant interpersonal skills. Rather, it was more likely to be assumed that the nonassertive individual was deficient in certain social skills, so that such skills must be taught.

Lamar worked at a city hospital in the file room. It was the lowest paid job in the hospital, but the only one that did not require him to talk to anyone.

He had had this job for about 2 years. He worked quietly by himself, took his breaks alone, and ate lunch in a corner of the cafeteria facing the wall. He lived in an efficiency apartment by himself and went out occasionally to a movie or to the YMCA. It took everything Lamar could muster to make an appointment at the local mental health clinic. He knew he had a problem, but the idea of talking to someone about it was terrifying. What finally drove Lamar to take some action was some unexpected bills on his car. He also knew that if he was ever to leave the file room and get a promotion, he would have to be able to interact with his coworkers and with patients at the hospital.

Lamar was enrolled in weekly group therapy at the clinic. The group had a strong social skills component, especially focusing on assertiveness skills. Lamar and others in the group found that their problems were not uniquely theirs and that many in the group suffered from social anxiety and skill deficits.

One of the defining characteristics of mentally retarded individuals has been their difficulties in social adjustment. Conversely, the ability to use appropriate social skills has been shown to be positively related to community and work adjustment among the developmentally disabled (cf. Andrasik & Matson, 1985). Whether such deficiencies in interpersonal skills are due to the person's inability to understand what is going on in social situations because of low IQ, or to some other reasons such as possible organic impairment or the coexistence of an emotional disorder, the fact remains that the lack of social skills is endemic in this population. In a time when the pressures for "normalization" have been most strongly felt by those working with the developmentally disabled, in part it is those interpersonal behaviors that society views as odd or abnormal that prevent mentally retarded individuals from truly entering the mainstream of society. For these reasons, social skills training has become an important component of treatment/training programs for the retarded. Indeed, social skills training programs may be particularly well suited because they tend to focus on concrete, clearly defined skills and do so in a stepwise, molecular way, allowing for considerable repetition and reinforcement throughout the process (Turner, Hersen, & Bellack, 1978). Individuals with severe intellectual, cognitive, and developmental impairments might well be seen in settings exclusively devoted to mental retardation, or they may find themselves intermingled with other diagnostic groups in community mental health settings. As suggested previously, some may carry dual diagnoses (e.g., mental retardation and psychosis).

Rose was about to enter the work force. She had been involved in a sheltered workshop for a long time, and it was believed that she could handle herself in a less sheltered setting. There was an opening at the local supermarket, and Rose's workshop supervisor decided to give it a try. Her job involved straightening up stock, sweeping, and dusting. Rose knew how to do all of these things.

The plan was to give Rose full-time supervision for the first month and then to taper that supervision once she became used to the job and the people. As it turned out, the job presented no problem. The people were a significant problem. Although the store managers were used to employees from the sheltered workshop, they frequently forgot to take the time to explain new tasks or to repeat instructions until they were understood.

Larry, Rose's supervisor, began a social skills program right at the market. He had four clients from the workshop, many of whom were having the same problem. The group met for a half hour each day, before going to the job placement. The focus was on those skills involving asking for help and following instructions. Larry even managed to enlist the assistance of one of the managers, so that when clients were practicing the skill of asking for help, they would practice asking this particular manager. The group was a great success. Not only did Rose (and others) learn how to verbalize their needs better in a work environment, but the manager was able to better understand how he needed to interact with this group of employees to make himself better understood.

The treatment of persons with substance abuse problems presents the greatest drain on society's mental-health-related resources. Professional publications, media portrayals, and pleas for help from families and personnel offices highlight the emotional and financial costs of substance abuse and dependency on a daily basis. Although mental health treatment settings are not the only places that individuals with drug or alcohol problems go or are sent for help, such problems are being seen with increased frequency. Substance abuse may be the primary disorder, or the person may also carry such psychiatric diagnoses as schizophrenia, depression, anxiety disorder (including posttraumatic stress disorder), and/or personality disorder. Indeed, one of the newest acronyms in the treatment lexicon is MICA (mentally ill chemical abuser), representing therapeutic challenges seldom encountered by mental health practitioners in the past.

Most of the treatment literature on substance abuse has dealt with alcohol, because of the longstanding recognition of the extent and severity of alcohol abuse and dependency. In recent years the need for treatment of those addicted to other drugs has been thrust on public awareness, sometimes borrowing from the alcohol treatment models and sometimes utilizing independent conceptualizations and treatment methodologies. What is so striking about both lay and professional views of the development of substance abuse problems and of their remediation is the explicit and implicit acknowledgement of the importance of social skills and social competencies. For example, Levine and Zigler (1973) found that alcoholism was much more likely to occur in persons who are judged to be deficient in social competencies. Problem drinkers may find it particularly difficult to establish social relationships (cf. O'Leary, O'Leary, & Donovan, 1976), perhaps never having learned such skills. They may use alcohol as a means of coping with difficult interpersonal situations. Alcohol (and perhaps other substances) may serve as an antianxiety agent, an antidepressant, and/or a social disinhibitor, but not always successfully and at a tremendous cost.

People who have been successful in overcoming their drug or alcohol addiction (and cigarette addiction) are highly likely to relapse. Marlatt and Gordon (1980) found a 70 to 80% relapse rate within 6 months after stopping alcohol, opiate, or cigarette use. Social pressures to resume drinking, drugging, or smoking and the lack of skills necessary to deal with these pressures (e.g., "drink refusal skills") are critical in relapses. Likewise, difficulties in interpersonal situations that the individual is not equipped to handle are also viewed as frequent risk factors in substance abuse relapse. After all, these substances were probably used and abused initially as attempts to cope with these types of difficult interpersonal situations.

The need for social skills training with individuals with substance abuse problems seems apparent. Such skills may help remedy the lack of social skills that may have led them to turn to alcohol or drugs. They may help prevent relapse once such persons have become abstinent; teaching assertive skills, drink refusal skills, or even basic conversational skills may be what can help make the difference between therapeutic success and failure for this high-risk population.

Jason dropped out of college right after his first semester. He did not even bother to take his exams. There were lots of alcohol and drugs on the campus, and he found that the only way he could face women and dormitory life was to stay stoned on something. The beer would loosen him up so that he could be witty and casual. Without a few drinks, he would be tongue-tied and would feel rather stupid. It all seemed like a great solution, until it got harder and harder to get out of bed to go to classes. It also got harder and harder to go a night without drinking, or to do homework, or to study for exams.

When Jason got home after failing that first semester, his parents quickly spotted the alcohol problem. Jason's father had been a heavy drinker in his younger years. He recognized the pattern repeating itself in Jason. He also recognized Jason's social anxiety and remembered in his own youth how alcohol seemed to "cure" the problem. A friend of the family recommended that Jason seek help through the substance abuse clinic connected with the university hospital. In addition to substance abuse counseling, Jason entered a group focused on social skills. Over the course of a number of months, he learned how to cope with his social anxiety without alcohol or drugs.

SUMMARY

Two converging trends have occurred in mental health treatments during the final third of the twentieth century. The large psychiatric institution was transformed and greatly diminished in size and scope, for both humanitarian and financial reasons. Initially there was widespread optimism that "the community" would absorb the burden of treatment for newly deinstitutionalized mental patients via a system of community mental health centers. But the chronic schizophrenics who left the mental hospitals were joined by a wide array of other patients and applicants for treatment who were never anticipated by early mental health planners. And while the community mental health centers were often expected to provide treatment, these diverse individuals were also making their complex needs known at other settings in the total support system: nursing homes, general hospitals, halfway houses, sheltered workshops, and prisons. Staff in all of these settings were typically ill-equipped to deal with the range of problems presented to them.

Social skills training developed initially in response to the treatment needs (seen as skill deficits) of chronic psychiatric patients. Both the need for social skills training to enhance social competencies and the techniques of social skills training were soon applied broadly to a wide range of applicants for mental health services in a variety of settings. At present, it is among the standard therapeutic offerings for persons with a spectrum of diagnoses, all of whom are viewed as deficient in important interpersonal skills.

Chapter 2

Structured Learning:
Background and
Development

The specific social skills training approach known as Structured Learning was developed in response to some of the needs of the newly deinstitutionalized psychiatric patients described in chapter 1. It grew out of learning theory and the behavior modification movement in psychology and has come to be referred to as a psychoeducational approach. In order to provide an understanding of the particular procedures and components that constitute Structured Learning, this chapter discusses some of the background research and rationale for their inclusion.

STRUCTURED LEARNING
COMPONENTS AND PROCEDURES

The four major components of Structured Learning are (1) modeling, (2) role playing, (3) performance feedback, and (4) transfer of training and maintenance. In groups that typically consist of four to eight or nine trainees and two trainers, participants are shown detailed examples of people (models) performing the interpersonal skills that are being taught (modeling). Trainees are then given the opportunity to rehearse or practice the skill that has been demonstrated in a situation relevant to their own lives (role playing). Next, feedback is provided, which includes encouragement and suggestions on ways that performance might be improved (performance feedback). Finally, they are exposed to procedures that are designed to increase the likelihood that the newly learned behaviors will be applied successfully and enduringly in their real-life environments (transfer of training and maintenance).

15

Modeling

The study of modeling, or imitative learning, has a long history in psychological research. Imitation has been examined under many names: copying, empathic learning, observational learning, identification, vicarious learning, matched-dependent behavior, and, most frequently, modeling. This body of research has shown that modeling is an effective, reliable, and rapid technique for both the teaching of new behaviors and the strengthening or weakening of behaviors that had been learned earlier. Three types of learning by modeling have been identified:

1. *Observational learning effects:* the learning of new behaviors that the person has never performed before. For example, many of the younger clients at mental health centers frequently appear in radically new styles of dress, which seem to change weekly, as do styles of talking, musical tastes, and folk heroes. Apparently influenced by mass media, these are examples of behaviors and attitudes acquired largely via observational learning.

2. *Inhibitory and disinhibitory effects:* the strengthening or weakening of behaviors that previously were performed very rarely by the person, because to do so would lead to disapproval or other negative reactions. For example, a client who is having difficulty with employment interviews because it is hard for her to talk about her own accomplishments ("bragging is bad") may be helped to become less inhibited by observing a model who is appropriately assertive and is successful in her job-seeking efforts.

3. *Behavior facilitation effects:* the performance of previously learned behaviors that are neither new nor the source of potential negative reactions from others. For instance, a clinic social worker frequently visits the homes of inner-city residents. He finds that the people he interviews provide fuller and more accurate information when they are relaxed. He has found that by modeling relaxed and friendly behavior, asking if he might sit down, explaining his purpose clearly in a nonthreatening and nonjudgmental manner, he is more likely to be responded to, in turn, in a relaxed and friendly manner by the people he is interviewing.

Research has shown an impressive variety and number of different behaviors that are learned, strengthened, weakened, or facilitated through modeling. These include acting aggressively, helping others, behaving independently, planning careers, becoming emotionally aroused, interacting socially, displaying dependency, exhibiting certain patterns of speech, behaving empathically, and self-disclosing, to mention only a few. Modeling is clearly an important and effective technique for teaching new behaviors.

Yet, it is also true that people are exposed to dozens, if not hundreds, of behaviors every day that they do not imitate. Every day they see and hear very polished and professional modeling displays, on television, magazines, and newspapers, urging them to buy one product or another. Yet, they do not purchase everything that is pitched at them. And many people observe expensively produced and expertly acted instructional films and videotapes, but they remain uninstructed. Apparently, people learn by modeling under some circumstances but not others. Laboratory research on modeling has identified a number of circumstances in which the effectiveness of modeling is likely to be greater. These are known as *modeling enhancers*. These modeling enhancers are the characteristics of the model, the modeling display, and/or the observer which have been shown to affect significantly the degree to which learning by imitation is likely to occur.

Modeling Enhancers.

1. *Model characteristics.* More effective modeling will occur when the model (the person to be imitated) (a) appears to be highly skilled or expert; (b) is of high status; (c) controls rewards desired by the observer; (d) is of the same sex, approximate age, and same race as the observer; (e) is apparently friendly and helpful; and, of particular importance, (f) is rewarded for the given behaviors. Thus, people are more likely to imitate expert or powerful but pleasant persons who resemble them in a number of ways and who receive rewards for what they are doing, especially when the particular rewards involved are things that are desired by them as well.

2. *Modeling display characteristics.* Modeling will be more effective when the modeling display shows the behaviors to be imitated (a) in a clear and detailed manner; (b) in the order from least difficult to most difficult behaviors; (c) with enough repetition to make overlearning likely; (d) with as little irrelevant detail as possible; and (e) when several different models, rather than a single model, are used.

3. *Observer characteristics.* More effective modeling will occur when the person observing the modeling (a) is told to imitate the model; (b) is similar to the model in background or in attitude toward the skill; (c) is friendly toward or likes the model; and, most important, (d) is rewarded for performing the modeled behaviors.

One's understanding of both the effects of these modeling enhancers as well as modeling itself can be made clearer by noting that learning by modeling involves three stages or phases.

Stages of Modeling.

1. *Attention.* An observer cannot learn from watching a model unless he or she pays attention to the modeling display and, in particular, to the specific behavioral steps that constitute the behavior being modeled. If these behavioral steps are buried in a large number of other stimuli, the likelihood of the observer paying attention to them may decrease. As noted earlier, one important modeling enhancer is minimizing irrelevant stimuli in the modeling display. Attention to and learning of the modeling display's behavioral steps are built into the display. Those few behaviors or steps that actually make up a given skill, and thus are displayed, must be shown in a vivid, real-life, and repetitive manner to maximize the likelihood that the observer will actually pay close attention to them. Similarly, the attention stage of modeling will be enhanced if the model is of high status, competent, and of the same sex, age, and race as the observer and is rewarded for performing the designated behavior.

2. *Retention.* In order to reproduce at a later time the behaviors that have been modeled, the observer must remember or retain them. Because the behaviors demonstrated in the modeling display are no longer present, retention must occur by memory. Memory is aided if the behaviors that have been modeled are classified or coded by the observer. Another name for such coding is "covert rehearsal"—i.e., reviewing in one's own mind the performance of the behaviors displayed. However, research has shown that even more important to retention than this mental covert rehearsal is overt behavioral rehearsal. Practice of the specific behavioral steps is crucial for learning and, indeed, constitutes the second major procedure of Structured Learning. This process is referred to as role playing and will be examined in depth shortly. It should be noted, however, that the likelihood of retention via either covert or overt rehearsal is aided by rewards being provided to both the model and/or the observer.

3. *Reproduction.* Researchers interested in human learning have typically drawn a distinction between learning (acquiring or gaining knowledge about how to do something) and performance (actually doing it). If the observer has paid attention to and remembered the behaviors shown in the modeling display, one may say that the person has learned those behaviors. However, the main concern is not whether the person can reproduce the behaviors that have been modeled, but whether he or she does reproduce them. As with retention, the likelihood that a person will perform a behavior that has been learned will depend mostly on the expectation of receiving a reward for having done so. Expectation of reward has been shown to be determined by the amount, consistency, recency, and frequency of the reward that the person has observed being

provided to the model for performing the desired behaviors. The crucial nature of reward for performance will be discussed further later in this chapter.

Research on Modeling. A great deal of research has been done over time on the effectiveness of modeling in real-life settings. For example, Lefkowitz, Blake, and Mouton (1954) examined the effect of a model on the frequency of pedestrian traffic violations. These researchers arranged to have an individual (the model) either cross a street or wait to cross during a period in which a "Wait" pedestrian traffic sign was lit. The imitative behavior (crossing or waiting) of over two thousand pedestrians was observed. The results indicated that significantly more pedestrians crossed against the "Wait" signal when the model crossed than when the model waited or when no model was present.

Research reported by Bryan and Test (1967) showed that not only may negative real-life behavior (traffic violations) be modeled, but positive, helpful behaviors as well. In their first research report, entitled "Lady in Distress," an automobile with a flat left-rear tire was parked on a busy Los Angeles street. A young woman was stationed by the car, and an inflated tire was leaned against the left side of the car. The car, the woman, the flat tire, and the spare tire were in clear view of the passing traffic. For 4 of the 8 hours that the experiment lasted, a second automobile was parked on the same street, one-quarter mile before the car described above. The car was raised by a jack under its left-rear bumper, and a young woman was watching a man (the model) changing a flat tire. This was the study's modeling procedure. The rest of the time, no such model was present. During the study, four thousand vehicles passed the two cars. Significantly more drivers stopped at the second car and offered to help the stranded motorist when the model was present than when the model was not present.

A second, similar study was conducted by the same researchers at a Princeton, New Jersey, shopping center. In this study, the procedure involved a model going up to a Salvation Army kettle, placing a donation in it, and walking away. Again, a modeling effect was shown; significantly more passersby made donations when the model had just done so.

Modeling has been used to change the behaviors of individuals in various types of interview situations. These studies ask whether one can increase interviewee self-disclosure, self-exploration, and progress toward interview goals by first showing a model engaged in such behaviors. Marlatt, Jacobson, Johnson, and Morrice (1970) reported a study in which 32 college students were each interviewed individually. They could talk in their interview about one or more problems out of three mentioned to them by the interviewer. Before the second interview, half of the interviewees listened to a tape-recorded interview in which the interviewee (model) revealed a great deal of personal information about the problem area that the listener had spoken about least in the first interview. The other half of the interviewees heard no such model. Results indicated that interviewees exposed to the problem-revealing model discussed that area significantly more in their second interviews than either they themselves had before or than those interviewees who had heard no model.

Liberman (1970) reported similar results in a study involving alcoholic patients in a psychiatric hospital. Before being interviewed, each patient listened to a tape recording in which a patient (model) answered several personal questions about his family, his feelings, his drinking, and so forth in either a highly self-disclosing manner or in a manner which revealed very little about himself. After hearing the tape, each patient was interviewed by the doctor who asked the same questions that had been put to the model on the tape. Patients who had heard the highly self-disclosing model revealed significantly more about themselves in this interview than did not only those who had heard a low self-disclosing model but also as compared to other patients who had heard either a neutral tape or no tape at all.

Other interview behaviors have been shown to be affected by modeling. Friedenberg (1971) and Walsh (1971) were able to increase interviewee liking for the interviewer; Krumboltz and Thoresen (1964) and Krumboltz, Varenhorst, and Thoresen (1967), working with career-planning interviews, were successful in increasing the degree to which interviewees sought out career information both during and after the interview; and studies by Matarazzo, Wiens, and Saslow (1965) made successful use of modeling to increase the sheer amount of interviewee talking.

In earlier investigations, modeling has also been shown to be effective in a number of additional areas relevant to a broad range of clinical concerns. Several studies have demonstrated the effectiveness of modeling to reduce fears or phobias. Kleinsasser (1968) reported success using modeling to help reduce anxiety about speaking before a group; Ritter (1969) was similarly successful in eliminating fear of heights; and Bandura, Blanchard, and Ritter (1969) helped subjects overcome intense fear of snakes. Modeling has also been shown to enhance hypnotizability. Klinger (1970) demonstrated that persons will be more easily hypnotized if they first observe a model displaying hypnotic behavior. Aggression, both its increase (Bandura, Ross, & Ross, 1961; Feshback, 1964) and its decrease (Chittenden, 1942) has long been shown to be influenced by modeling procedures. Certainly relevant to the effectiveness of clinical activities are the attitudes and behaviors of health care providers, which have also been shown to be influenced through modeling (Goldstein, 1973).

More recent research has continued to demonstrate the potency of observational learning interventions, employed alone or in diverse combination treatment packages, to alter a wide array of both deviant and prosocial behaviors. These have included effective parenting behaviors (Mastria, Mastria, & Harkins, 1979), self-control (Kendall & Braswell, 1982), employment skills (Hall, Loeb, Coyne, & Cooper, 1981), empathy and helping behaviors (Radke-Yarrow, Zahn-Waxler, & Chapman, 1983), and the modeling of a variety of other behaviors relevant to such settings as the home (Gambrill, 1983), the community (Schnelle, Geller, & Davis, 1987), closed institutions (Milan, 1987), and elsewhere (Deguchi, 1984).

Modeling—Necessary but Insufficient. The positive outcomes of these representative modeling studies may raise questions about the need for the other components of Structured Learning. If so many types of behaviors have been changed so successfully by watching a model, why are role playing, performance feedback, and transfer of training and maintenance necessary? The answer is clear: modeling alone is not enough because its many positive effects are very often short-lived. For example, ministers who were taught (by modeling) to be more empathic when conducting interviews were indeed more empathic immediately after training, but a very short time later their increased empathic ability had disappeared (Perry, 1970). A modeling study of empathy with nurses and hospital aides produced the same result (Sutton, 1970). Earlier it was noted that learning appears to be improved when the learner has an opportunity and is encouraged to practice, rehearse, or role play the behaviors that have been observed and is rewarded for so doing. In other words, viewing the modeling display teaches the observer what to do. In addition, the observer needs enough practice to learn how to do it and sufficient reward to provide motivation—to answer the question of why it is worthwhile to perform the behaviors that are being taught. Before addressing the why, it is important to discuss the how: role playing, the second component of Structured Learning.

Role Playing

Role playing has been defined as "a situation in which an individual is asked to take a role [behave in certain ways] not normally his own, or if his own, in a place not normal for the enactment of the role" (Mann, 1956). The use of role playing, acting, behavioral rehearsal, and similar methods to help a person change behavior or attitudes has been a popular approach for many years.

Role playing has been the target of a considerable amount of research, much of it aimed at studying the effects of role playing on attitude change. In the typical experiment of this type, the research subjects are first given some sort of attitude questionnaire. One of the attitude dimensions on this questionnaire is selected for the study. The subjects are then assigned to one of three experimental groups. Those placed in the role-play group are requested to make a speech or other public statement on the attitude dimension, in support of attitudes that are opposite to those they really believe. That is, they must defend publicly and actively a viewpoint that is contrary to their own views. Subjects in the second group, the exposure group, hold the same private attitudes as the role-play subjects but are not asked to make a public statement opposite to their real beliefs, but simply required to listen to one of the speeches made by a role-play subject. Control group subjects neither make nor hear such speeches. All subjects are then given the attitude questionnaire a second time. This type of experiment has shown consistently that role-playing subjects change their attitudes (away from what they believed privately, toward what they said publicly) significantly more than either exposure or control group subjects.

Studies such as these form an impressive demonstration of the value of role playing in bringing about attitude and behavior change. However, as was noted earlier in discussing modeling, behavior and attitude change through role playing will occur and endure only if certain conditions are met. Behavior or attitude change through role playing either will not occur or will not be lasting if the role player does not have enough information about the content of the role to enact it (or if such information has not been shown by a model) and if insufficient attention has been given to what may be called *role-play enhancers*. Role-play enhancers, like modeling enhancers, are procedures that increase the likelihood of lasting behavior change. Specifically, behavior change through role playing will be greater and more lasting the greater the role player's

1. choice regarding whether to take part in the role playing;
2. commitment to the behavior or behavior being role played, in the sense that the enactment is public rather than private, or is otherwise difficult to disown;
3. improvisation in enacting the role-played behaviors; and
4. reinforcement, approval, or reward for enacting the role-played behaviors.

Research on Role Playing. One rather dramatic early use of role playing is a study conducted by Janis and Mann (1965) aimed at decreasing smoking. Their research subjects were 26 young women who were all smokers. Their attitudes toward stopping smoking and the number of cigarettes each smoked per day were recorded at the beginning of the study. The subjects were asked to assume that they were medical patients who had just undergone a series of diagnostic tests and were awaiting the results. The experimenter took the part of a physician. Half of the women were asked to play the role of patient (role players) and the other 13 "patients" (listeners) listened to tape recordings of the role players. The role players then individually acted five scenes with the "physician," all of which were designed to arouse fear. The first scene took place in the waiting room. The role player was encouraged to express fear regarding the outcome of the diagnostic procedures. Scene two involved a conversation with the "physician" at which time she learned that she had lung cancer and that surgery was necessary. During the third scene, she expressed concern about the diagnosis; during scene four, she discussed the hospital arrangements and the moderate likelihood of a successful outcome. The fifth scene involved a conversation with the "physician" about the relationship between smoking and lung cancer. Attitude measurement and number of cigarettes smoked per day were recorded again. Results indicated that the role players' attitudes about the smoking–lung cancer relationship and willingness to try to stop smoking changed significantly more than did the listeners' attitudes. Furthermore, and of greater importance from a behavioral viewpoint, the role players were actually smoking significantly fewer cigarettes per day.

A second impressive demonstration of the effects of role playing was reported by McFall and Marston (1970). They worked with 42 people who felt that they were too unassertive and dependent. The purpose of the role playing was to increase their assertive and independent behaviors. The researchers developed 24 situations which the subject was asked to listen to and then respond by role playing what an assertive person might say and do. For example, in one situation each subject heard:

Narrator: Imagine that this morning you took your car to a local Standard station, and you explicitly told the mechanic to give you a simple tune-up. The bill should have been about $20. It is now later in the afternoon, and you're at the station to pick up your car. The mechanic is walking over to you.

Mechanic: Okay, let me make out a ticket for you. The tune-up was $12 for parts and $8 for labor. Uh, grease and oil job was $6. Antifreeze was $5. Uh, $4 for a new oil filter, and uh, $5 for rotating the tires. That's $40 in all. Will this be cash or charge?

Subjects were encouraged and helped to role play assertive responses to the situations. They were given coaching on their directness, tone of voice, inflection, communication of feeling, and so forth. After completion of these procedures, role players were compared on several measures of assertiveness with other subjects who had discussed but had not role played being more assertive and others who had neither role played nor discussed assertiveness. The role players were not only more assertive on these measures but were significantly less anxious about being assertive. McFall and Marston, furthermore, tried to find out if the role-play training had any effect on the assertiveness of subjects in their real-life behavior. Two weeks after their role-play participation, each subject was telephoned by another experimenter posing as a magazine salesperson. Working from a prepared script, the "salesperson" delivered a hard-sell pitch for magazine subscriptions. The telephone call was terminated only (1) after the subject agreed to buy, (2) after 5 minutes had passed without a sale, (3) after all sales gambits had been used without success, or (4) after the subject had hung up on the "salesperson." Analysis of these telephone conversations revealed that the subjects who had undergone the role playing showed strong sales resistance at a significantly earlier point in the telephone call than did both other groups of subjects.

The two investigations just described—of smoking and of assertiveness—are similar to the use of role playing in Structured Learning because they are both clearly behavioral targets. However, most research on role playing has focused on attitude, not behavior change. Culbertson (1957) sought to learn if attitudes toward integration in housing could be changed by role playing. Her research subjects were 95 adults whose attitudes toward racial integration she measured, whom she then divided into three groups:

1. *Role players*. These subjects were required to enact three roles in favor of the use of educational programs to prevent or reduce tension and antagonism in a community about to be integrated.
2. *Observers*. These subjects listened to the role play but did not role play themselves.
3. *Controls*. These subjects completed the attitude measures (pre and post), as did role players and observers, but neither role played nor observed any role playing. Results of this investigation indicated significantly greater attitude change in pro-integration among role players than either observers or controls.

Using the same or similar experimental procedures, role players have shown significantly more attitude change than observers or controls on such other attitude dimensions as the sale and use of alcohol (Harvey & Beverly, 1961), attitudes toward another person (Davis & Jones, 1960), the value of compulsory religious education (Cohen & Latane, 1962), attitudes toward the police (Brehm & Cohen, 1962), moral judgment (Arbuthnot, 1975), conflict management skills (Spivack & Shure, 1974), altruism (Iannotti, 1977), empathy (Staub, 1971), and a variety of other social skills (Rathjen, Hiniker, & Rathjen, 1976; Ross, Ross, & Evans, 1976). This small sample of early investigations of the consequences of role-play participation demonstrates that such involvement can lead to many types of attitude and behavior change, a general finding amply reconfirmed in more recent studies evaluating the impact of role playing alone or in diverse combinations (Calabrese & Hawkins, 1988; Clark, Christoff, & Hansen 1986; Hierholzer & Liberman, 1986; Hollin & Trower, 1988; Jamison, Lambert, & McCloud, 1985; Mueser & Liberman, 1988; Mueser, Valenti-Hein, & Yarnold, 1987; Plienis et al., 1987; Stravynski, Grey, & Elie, 1987; Wildman, Wildman, & Kelly, 1986).

Role Playing—Necessary but Insufficient. Thus far, considerable evidence has been presented supporting the value of role-playing procedures in a variety of settings. As with modeling, role playing has been shown to be a necessary but insufficient condition for bringing about lasting behavioral change. When used alone, like the effects of modeling when used alone, its effects seem to vanish fairly quickly. Three investigations reported by Lichtenstein, Keutzer, and Himes (1969) on the effects of role playing on smoking failed to demonstrate any lasting behavioral change. Furthermore, a study reported by Hollander (1970) found no behavioral change due to role playing, even though choice, commitment, improvisation, and reward were all reflected in her procedures. Thus, in most attempts to help a person change behavior, neither modeling alone nor role playing alone is enough. Combining the two is an improvement, because then the person knows what to do and how to do it. But even this combination is insufficient because the person still needs to know why he or she should behave in new ways. That is, a motivational or incentive component must be added to the "training package." It is for this purpose that performance feedback now needs to be considered.

Performance Feedback

Performance feedback, within the context of Structured Learning, is defined in terms of providing the participant with information on how well he or she is doing, particularly during the role playing. Such information generally takes the form of reward, constructive criticism, reteaching, or, most often, social reinforcement (i.e., praise, encouragement, approval). The nature and effects of reinforcement have received more study than any other aspect of the learning process. Indeed, reinforcement has been shown to be a particularly potent influence on behavioral change.

Reinforcement has typically been defined as any event that serves to increase the likelihood that a given behavior will occur. Three types of reinforcement have been described: (1) material reinforcement, such as food or money, (2) social reinforcement, such as praise or approval from others, and (3) self-reinforcement, which is the person's positive evaluation of his or her own behavior. Effective training must give proper attention to all three types of reinforcement. Material reinforcement may be viewed as a necessary base, without which "higher" levels of reinforcement (social and self) may not function. For many people, especially chronic psychiatric patients and mentally retarded individuals, material reinforcement may be the only class of reinforcement to which they will respond at first. This notion underlies the development of token economies in mental hospitals and some community-based settings. But there is considerable evidence that, although patients may change as a function of token rewards, such changed behavior typically disappears (extinguishes) when the tokens are no longer forthcoming. It is for this reason that an effort is usually made within token economies to pair social reinforcement with material reinforcement, and eventually to have the former substitute for the latter. In real-life settings, a job well done (if it receives any reward at all) receives a verbal "nice job" more often than a tangible reward, and helping a friend with a chore elicits "thanks" or approval, not money or objects. Stated otherwise, it is important that a skill training effort not rely too heavily or too long on material reinforcers.

Even though social reinforcers may be more likely and hence more valuable than material reinforcers in a real-life sense, it is also true that many valuable real-life behaviors go unnoticed, uncommented on, and unappreciated by others. Therefore, social reinforcement, too, may be an unreliable ally in the skill training enterprise. Because of their own needs and reasons, such potential social reinforcement dispensers as hospital or clinic staff, relatives, and friends may often be either nonrewarding or simply unavailable. However, if social skills teachers can aid participants in becoming their own reinforcement suppliers, if these teachers can help clients evaluate their skill behaviors and to praise or approve their effective performances, then a major stride will have been made toward increasing the likelihood that the newly learned skills will be performed in a reliable and enduring way where they will make a difference—at home, at work, or in other real-life settings.

Thus far, reinforcement has been defined, the nature and consequences of different types of reinforcement have been indicated, and its importance for human performance has been emphasized. In looking for effective training methods, it is insufficient to simply acknowledge that reinforcement is a crucial ingredient in the training process; the effectiveness and endurance of the influence of reinforcement on performance will depend on several characteristics of the reinforcements used. It is these characteristics, or *reinforcement enhancers*, that will now be examined.

Reinforcement Enhancers.

1. *Type of reinforcement.* As McGehee and Thayer (1961) observed, "What one person regards as a rewarding experience may be regarded by another as neutral or non-rewarding, or even punishing" (p. 140). Whereas it is obviously true that certain types of reinforcers such as approval, food, affection, and money have a high likelihood of serving as effective rewards for most people most of the time, this will not always be the case. Both the individual's reinforcement history and needs at the time will affect whether the intended reinforcer is in fact reinforcing. Therefore, it is desirable that all training procedures take into account and respond to the individual reinforcement histories and current needs of the participants. This means choosing not only between giving material, social, and self-reinforcers when necessary but also making changes in these selections in a continuing and sensitive manner.

2. *Delay of reinforcement.* Laboratory research on learning has shown consistently that behavior change occurs most effectively when the reinforcement follows immediately after the desired behavior. Reinforcement strengthens the behavior that was going on immediately preceding the dispensing of the reward and makes it more likely that the behavior will occur again. Thus, it is possible that delayed reinforcement can lead to the strengthening of inappropriate or ineffective behaviors if such behaviors occur between the desired behavior and the onset of reinforcement. This may be of less danger than it seems, however, because people usually remember why they are being reinforced or rewarded. As Bandura (1969) noted, "A person who is paid on a piecework basis is likely to maintain a high performance level, although he receives his total payment at the end of the month rather than in small amounts immediately after each unit of work is completed" (pp. 231–232).

3. *Response-contingent reinforcement.* Related to the issue of immediate versus delayed reinforcement are other matters of timing which help

or hinder the effects of reinforcement on performance. Bandura (1969) commented:

> In many instances considerable rewards are bestowed, but they are not made conditional upon the behavior that change agents wish to promote . . . special privileges, activities, and rewards are generally furnished according to fixed time schedules rather than performance requirements, and, in many cases, positive reinforcers are inadvertently made contingent upon the wrong types of behavior. (pp. 229–230)

Thus, it is clear that the contingent relationship or linkage between performance and reinforcement, must be reflected in training procedures and made sufficiently clear to the participant.

4. *Amount and quality of reinforcement.* In addition to the considerations already noted concerning the type, timing, and contingency of the reinforcement provided, the amount and quality of the reinforcement will be a major source of its effect on performance. With certain important exceptions, the greater the amount of reinforcement, the greater the positive effect on performance. One limitation on this principle is that increases in certain types of reinforcement do increase performance, but in smaller and smaller amounts. Research on amount of reinforcement serves as further illustration of the difference between learning and performance. In the laboratory, at least, subjects appear to learn (acquire new knowledge) no more rapidly for large rewards than for small ones. Once learning has taken place, however, performance often will be more dependable if larger rewards are provided.

5. *Opportunity for reinforcement.* A further requirement for successful and consistent performance is that the behavior to be reinforced must occur with sufficient frequency that reinforcement can be provided. If such behaviors are too infrequent, insufficient opportunity will exist to influence them through contingent reinforcement. It is also true that beyond its several types of practice effects noted earlier, role playing provides excellent opportunities to provide appropriate contingent reinforcement.

6. *Partial (intermittent) reinforcement.* Partial reinforcement refers to the reinforcement of only some of the person's correct responses by rewarding at fixed times (e.g., once every 5 minutes), at a fixed number of responses (e.g., every fifth correct response), on a variable time or response schedule (e.g., randomly choosing, within limits, the time or correct response to reward), and on other schedules. In all instances, it has been shown consistently that responses acquired under conditions of partial reinforcement are exceedingly resistant to extinction. That is, they continue to occur even when they are not reinforced at all.

In summary of the discussion of reinforcement thus far, research evidence combines to indicate that high levels of performance are likely to occur if the participant is given enough opportunity to receive immediate reinforcement that is individually tailored, in sufficiently large amounts, and offered on a response-contingent basis on an intermittent schedule. The following small sample of research investigations is presented to highlight these conclusions.

Research on Reinforcement. Verbal behavior—how much a person speaks, what a person says, and how a person says it—has long been the target of research on human reinforcement, especially social reinforcement. Verplanck (1955) proposed that when two people are having a conversation, and one person agrees with or paraphrases the opinions stated by the other person, such agreement or paraphrasing should serve as a reinforcement. If this is the case, the rate of stating opinions should increase. To test this hypothesis, Verplanck and 17 experimenters conducted half-hour conversations with a total of 24 subjects. During the first 10 minutes of each half-hour conversation, the experimenter neither agreed with nor paraphrased any opinion statements offered by the subject. During the second 10 minutes, every opinion statement by the subject was responded to by the experimenter who either agreed with it ("Yes," "You're right," "That's so," nodding, smiling, etc.) or paraphrasing it. During the last 10 minutes of each conversation, agreement and paraphrasing were again withheld. If Verplanck's prediction was correct that agreement and paraphrasing are indeed social reinforcers, subjects should have increased opinion statements during the second phase of each conversation and decreased such statements during the third phase, when the presumed reinforcement was withheld. Analysis of the 24 conversations, which were held in public and private places and covered a broad range of topics, revealed significant support for the predictions. Every reinforced subject increased in rate of offering opinions, whereas 21 of the 24 decreased in rate with nonreinforcement.

Related findings, also showing the ability of reinforcement to alter verbal behavior, were reported by Hildum and Brown (1956). In an attitude survey conducted by telephone, they predicted that the use of the word "good" by the interviewer would serve as a reinforcer and, therefore, change the interviewee's statements. During half of the calls made, the interviewer answered with "good" to interviewee statements that agreed with the attitude issue; during the other calls, the interviewer responded the same way to disagreeing statements. A significant difference emerged between the two groups. Those reinforced for agreeing became more agreeable, and those reinforced for disagreeing increased their disagreement. This study was later replicated with similar results.

Many other investigations have shown that reinforcement can increase, decrease, or otherwise alter what subjects say, their opinions and attitudes, and a wide range of other behaviors. More specifically, behaviors shown to be changed by reinforcement include remembering personal experiences (Quay, 1959), expressions of feeling (Salzinger & Pisoni, 1957), evaluations of other people (Gelfand & Singer, 1968), acceptance of self (Nuthman, 1957), social interaction (Milby, 1970), and many more. In studies such as these, the words or actions shown to serve as effective social reinforcers have included "good," "mm-hmm," "fine," "all right," "I see," head nodding, smiling, and leaning forward.

A considerable amount of evidence has been presented that supports the behavior change impact of modeling, role playing, and reinforcement. We have held that neither modeling alone nor role playing alone yields results nearly as effective as the two combined. A similar position also appears warranted regarding reinforcement. Whereas it is true that reinforcement alone is more likely to lead to lasting behavior change than either modeling or role playing alone, it is also true that the behaviors to be reinforced must occur with sufficient correctness and sufficient frequency for reinforcement to have its intended effect. Modeling can provide correctness; role playing can provide the frequency. Yet, there is one further component of Structured Learning to be considered, which is responsive to the massive failures of gains made either in training programs or in psychotherapies to transfer from the training site or the clinic office to real-life settings where they are likely to have positive impacts on participants' lives. In many ways, the issue of transfer of training and of maintaining such gains is the most important consideration in any psychotherapeutic or psychoeducational endeavor.

Transfer of Training and Maintenance

The main interest of any training or treatment program (and where most training and treatment programs fail) is not the participants' performance in the training site but, instead, how well they perform in their real lives. If skills have been learned and performed satisfactorily at the time of the training or treatment, what procedures are available to maximize the chances that such performance will continue in a durable manner at home, at work, or in the community? Stated otherwise, how can transfer of training and maintenance be encouraged?

Research has identified a number of principles of transfer and maintenance enhancement, the most potent of which will now be examined. Although it may prove difficult to implement all of these principles in any given training program, their combined impact will increase greatly the likelihood of satisfactory positive transfer and maintenance.

Transfer-enhancing Techniques.

1. *Provision of general principles.* Transfer of training may be facilitated by providing the participant with the general mediating principles that govern satisfactory performance on both the original and transfer tasks. The trainee can be given rules, strategies, or organizing principles that lead to successful performance. This general finding, that mediating principles for successful performance can enhance transfer to new tasks and contexts, has been reported in a number of domains of psychological research. These include studies of labeling, rules, advance organizers, learning sets, and deutero-learning. It is a robust finding indeed, with empirical support in both laboratory (Duncan, 1953, 1958; Goldbeck, Bernstein, Hellix, & Marx, 1957; Hendrickson & Schroeder, 1941; Ulmer, 1939) and clinical psychoeducational settings—the latter including the scripted roles in Kelly's (1955) fixed role therapy; directives in Haley's (1976) problem-solving therapy; strategies in Phillips' (1956) assertion-structured therapy; principles in MacGregor, Ritchie, Serrano, and Schuster's (1964) multiple impact therapy; problem-solving skills in Steiner et al.'s (1975) radical therapy; and in many of the self-regulatory, mediational interventions that lie at the heart of cognitive behavior therapy (Kanfer & Karoly, 1972; Kendall & Braswell, 1985).

2. *Overlearning.* Transfer of training has been shown to be enhanced by procedures that maximize overlearning or response availability; the likelihood that a response will be available is very clearly a function of its prior usage. One repeats and repeats foreign language phrases he or she is trying to learn, parents insist that their child practice the piano daily, and athletes devote considerable time practicing to make their golf swings smooth and automatic. These examples are simply the expressions of the response availability notion: that is, the more one has practiced (especially correct) responses, the easier it will be to use them in other contexts or at later times. One need not rely solely on everyday experience. It has been well established empirically that, other things being equal, the response that has been emitted most frequently in the past is more likely to be emitted on subsequent occasions. This finding is derived from studies of the frequency of evocation hypothesis and the spew hypothesis (Underwood & Schultz, 1960), preliminary response pretraining (Atwater, 1953; Cantor, 1955; Gagne & Foster, 1949), and overlearning (Mandler, 1954; Mandler & Heinemann, 1956). In all of these related research domains, real-life or laboratory-induced prior familiarization with given responses increased the likelihood of their occurrence on later trials. Mandler (1954) summarized much of this

research as it bears on transfer by noting that "learning to make an old response to a new stimulus showed increasing positive transfer as the degree of original training was increased" (p. 412). Mandler's studies of overlearning are especially relevant to our present theme because it is not sheer practice of attempts at prosocially effective behaviors that is of benefit to transfer, it is practice of successful attempts.

Overlearning involves extending learning over more trials than are necessary merely to produce initial changes in the individual's behavior. In all too many instances of near successful training, one or two successes at a given task are taken as evidence to move on to the next task or the next level of the original task. This is a training technique error if one wishes to maximize transfer via overlearning. Mandler's (1954) subjects were trained on the study task until they were able to perform it without error (0, 10, 30, 50, or 100 consecutive times). As noted earlier, transfer varied with the degree of original learning. To maximize transfer through the use of this principle, the guiding rule should not be "practice makes perfect" (implying that one simply practices until one gets it right and then moves on), but " practice of perfect" (implying numerous over-learning trials of correct responses after the initial success).

3. *Stimulus variability.* In the previous section we addressed enhancement of transfer by means of practice and repetition; that is, by the sheer number of correct responses the trainee makes to a given stimulus. Transfer is also enhanced by the variability or range of stimuli to which the individual responds. For example, Duncan (1958) has shown that, on paired-associates tasks, transfer is markedly enhanced by varied training. Training on even only two stimuli is better than training on a single stimulus. Other investigators have obtained similar results in concept attainment tasks, showing more rapid attainment when a variety of examples is presented (Callantine & Warren, 1955; Shore & Sechrest, 1961). As Kazdin (1975) commented:

> One way to program response maintenance and transfer of training is to develop the target behavior in a variety of situations and in the presence of several individuals. If the response is associated with a range of settings, individuals, and other cues, it is less likely to be lost when the situations change. (p. 21)

Stimulus variability has only a modest history of use in clinical and psychoeducational contexts thus far. For example, multiple-impact therapy for MacGregor et al. (1964); use of multiple therapists by Dreikurs, Schulman, and Mosak (1952), Hayward, Peters, and Taylor (1952), and Whitaker, Malone, and Warkentin (1966); round-robin therapy (Holmes, 1971); and rotational group therapy (Frank, 1973; Slavin, 1967). In the clinical realm of anger management, Feindler and Ecton (1986) urged the employment of stimulus variability (varied task training) for transfer enhancement purpose through the use of diverse role-play stimulus situations.

4. *Identical elements.* In perhaps the earliest experimental work dealing with transfer enhancement, Thorndike and Woodworth (1901) concluded that when there was a facilitative effect of one habit on another, it was to the extent that, and because, habits shared identical elements. Ellis (1965) and Osgood (1953) have more recently emphasized the importance for transfer of similarity between characteristics of the training and application tasks. As Osgood (1953) noted, "the greater the similarity between practice and test stimuli, the greater the amount of positive transfer" (p. 213). This conclusion rests on a particularly solid base of experimental support, involving studies of both motor (Crafts, 1935; Duncan, 1953; Gagne, Baker, & Foster, 1950) and verbal behaviors (Osgood, 1949, 1953; Underwood, 1951; Young & Underwood, 1954).

In the contexts of psychotherapy and psychoeducational training, the principle of identical elements could be implemented by procedures that function to increase the "real-lifeness" of the stimuli (people, places, behaviors, events, etc.) to which the therapist or trainer is helping the target person learn to respond. There exist two broad strategies for attaining such high levels of similarity between in-therapy and extra-therapy stimuli. The first is to move the training or therapy out of the typical office setting and into the very interpersonal and physical context in which the person's real-life difficulties are being experienced. Such in vivo interventions are, in fact, a growing reality. The locus of at least some approaches has shifted to homes, planes, bars, elevators, and other problem sites (Sherman, 1979; Sherman & Levine, 1979). To be sure, marital and family therapies are all examples of use of identical elements in the interpersonal sense, because the persons treated and the persons to whom they must apply their therapeutic learnings are one and the same.

The second broad approach to maximizing identical elements, or as Epps, Thompson, and Lane (1985) put it, programming common stimuli, is to remain in a training setting but to enhance its physical and/or interpersonal real-lifeness. This is done regularly within the context of Structured Learning groups by creating role plays that appear like and feel like "the real thing" (Goldstein, Sprafkin, Gershaw, & Klein, 1980). Transitional living centers and the systematic use of "barbs" (Epps et al., 1985) or "red flags" (McGinnis & Goldstein, 1984) in classroom settings are examples of promoting transfer by maximizing identical elements.

5. *Mediated generalization.* The one certain common element that is present in both training and application settings is the individual target trainee. Mediated generalization is an approach to transfer enhancement that relies on instructing the trainee in a series of context-bridging, self-

regulation competencies (Kanfer & Karoly, 1972; Neilans & Israel, 1981). Operationally, it consists of instructing the trainee in self-recording, self-reinforcement, self-punishment, and self-instruction. Epps et al. (1985), working in a special education setting, have structured these generalization-mediating steps as follows:

Self-recording
1. The teacher sets up the data collection system; that is, selects a target behavior, defines it in measurable terms, and decides on an appropriate recording technique.
2. The teacher tries out the data collection system.
3. The teacher teaches the trainee how to use the data collection system.
4. The teacher reinforces the trainee for taking accurate data.

Self-reinforcement
1. The teacher determines how many points a trainee has earned, and the trainee simply records these.
2. The teacher tells the trainee to decide how many points should be awarded for appropriate behavior.
3. The trainee practices self-reinforcement under teacher supervision.
4. The trainee uses self-reinforcement without teacher supervision.

Self-punishment
Self-punishment, operationalized in this example by response-cost (taking points away), is taught in a manner directly parallel to that just described for self-reinforcement, in which the teacher uses the technique of fading (gradually reducing the response-cost).

Self-instruction
1. The teacher models the appropriate behavior while talking him- or herself through the task out loud so that the trainee can hear.
2. The trainee performs the task with overt instructions from the teacher.
3. The trainee performs the task with overt self-instructions.
4. The trainee performs the task with covert self-instructions.

As the cognitive behavior modification therapies have grown in popularity in recent years, especially those relying heavily on self-instructional processes, self-mediated approaches to generalization have grown correspondingly in frequency of use.

Maintenance-enhancing Techniques. The persistence, durability, or maintenance of behaviors developed by diverse skills training approaches·is primarily a matter of the manipulation of reinforcement both during the original training and in the postintervention, real-world context. There are several specific means by which such maintenance-enhancing manipulation of reinforcement may proceed.

1. *Thinning of reinforcement.* A rich, continuous reinforcement schedule is optimal for the establishment of new behaviors. Maintenance of such behaviors will be enhanced if the reinforcement schedule is gradually thinned. Thinning of reinforcement will proceed best by moving from a continuous (all trials) schedule to another form of intermittent schedule to the level of sparse and infrequent reinforcement characteristic of the natural environment. In fact, the maintenance-enhancing goal of such a thinning process is to make the trainer-offered reinforcement schedule indistinguishable from that typically offered in real-world contexts.

2. *Delay of reinforcement.* Resistance to extinction is also enhanced by delay of reinforcement. As Epps et al. (1985) noted:

> During the early stages of an intervention, reinforcement should be immediate and continuously presented contingent on the desired response. . . . After the behavior becomes firmly established in the student's repertoire, it is important to introduce a delay in presenting the reinforcement. Delayed reinforcement is a closer approximation to reinforcement conditions in the natural environment. (p. 21)

According to Sulzer-Azaroff and Mayer (1977), delay of reinforcement may be implemented by (a) increasing the size or complexity of the response required before reinforcement is provided, (b) adding a time delay between the response and the delivery of the reinforcement, and (c) in token systems, increasing the time interval between receiving tokens and the opportunity to spend them and/or requiring more tokens in exchange for a given reinforcer.

3. *Fading of prompts.* Maintenance may be enhanced by the gradual removal of suggestions, reminders, prompts, or similar coaching or instruction. Fading of prompts is a means of moving away from artificial control (the trainer's) to more natural (self) control of desirable behaviors. As with all of the enhancement techniques examined here, fading of prompts should be planned carefully and implemented systematically.

4. *Booster training sessions.* Notwithstanding the importance of fading of prompts, it may be necessary periodically to reinstate instruction in the specifics of given appropriate behaviors in order for those behaviors to continue in the natural environment. Booster or review sessions, either on a preplanned schedule or as needed, have often proved quite valuable in this regard (Feindler & Ecton, 1986; Karoly & Steffen, 1980).

5. *Preparation for natural environment nonreinforcement.* Both trainer and trainee may take several energetic steps to maximize the likelihood that reinforcement for appropriate behaviors will occur in the natural

environment. Nevertheless, on a number of occasions, reinforcement will not be forthcoming. Thus, it is important for maintenance purposes that the trainee be prepared for this eventuality. As described in the earlier examination of mediated generalization, self-reinforcement is one means of responding in a maintenance-promoting manner when the desirable behaviors are performed correctly but are unrewarded by external sources. When trainees perform the behaviors incorrectly or inappropriately in the natural environment, they will respond best to the environment's nonreinforcement if they have previously learned skills and cognitive interpretations for dealing with relapse and failure experiences. Kendall and Braswell (1985) have proposed means for implementing this suggestion. An additional way in which the trainee may be prepared for nonreinforcement in the natural environment, at least in the context of social skills training and similar interventions, is the use of graduated homework assignments. In the Structured Learning approach, for example, skills role played successfully within group sessions are assigned as homework to be performed outside of the group. The trainee's task is to perform the skill before the next session with a real-life parent, spouse, or neighbor. On occasion, it becomes clear as the homework is discussed that the real-life figure is too difficult a target—too harsh, too unresponsive, or simply too unlikely to provide reinforcement for competent skill use. When faced with this circumstance, with the newly learned skill still fragile and the potential homework environment looming as nonrewarding, trainers have recast the homework assignment toward two or three more benevolent and more responsive target figures. When the trainee finally does use the skill correctly with the original target figure and receives no positive reinforcement, his or her string of previously reinforced trials helps minimize the likelihood that the behavior will be extinguished.

6. *Programming for reinforcement in the natural environment.* The maintenance-enhancing techniques examined thus far are targeted toward the trainee's reinforcement schedule, instruction, booster sessions, and preparation for nonreinforcing consequences, but maintenance of appropriate behaviors also may be enhanced by efforts directed toward others, especially those others in the natural environment who function as the main providers of reinforcement. As Galassi and Galassi (1984) commented:

> Significant others can be trained to deliver the same or similar contingencies in the natural environment as occurred during treatment. Parents, peers, and teachers can be taught to apply reinforcement for appropriate behavior. . . . Perhaps even better than individuals being taught new behaviors in a treatment setting by professionals and later having significant others trained to ensure transfer to the natural environment, is

training significant others initially to conduct the entire training process in the natural environment. (p. 12)

Patterson and Brodsky (1966), Nay (1979); Tharp and Wetzel (1969); and Walker, Hops, and Johnson (1975) are among the several investigators who have demonstrated repeatedly the efficacy of this now generally used approach to maintenance enhancement.

7. *Using natural reinforcers.* A final and especially valuable approach to maintenance enhancement is the use of reinforcers that naturally and readily exist in the trainee's real-world environment. Stokes and Baer (1977) observed:

> Perhaps the most dependable of all generalization programming mechanisms is the one that hardly deserves the name; the transfer of behavioral control from the teacher-experimenter to stable, natural contingencies that can be trusted to operate in the environment to which the subject will return, or already occupies. To a considerable extent, this goal is accomplished by choosing behaviors to teach that normally will meet maintaining reinforcement after the teaching. (p. 353)

Galassi and Galassi (1984) offered the following similar comment:

> We need to target those behaviors for changes that are most likely to be seen as acceptable, desirable, and positive by others. Ayllon and Azrin (1968) refer to this as the "Relevance of Behavior Rule." "Teach only those behaviors that will continue to be reinforced after training." (p. 10)

Alberto and Troutman (1982) suggested a four-step process that facilitates effective use of natural reinforcers: (a) observe which specific behaviors are regularly reinforced and how they are reinforced in the major settings that constitute the trainee's natural environment; (b) instruct the trainee in a selected number of such naturally reinforced behaviors (e.g., certain social skills, grooming behaviors); (c) teach the trainee how to recruit or request reinforcement (e.g., by tactfully asking peers or others for approval or recognition); and (d) teach the trainee how to recognize reinforcement when it is offered because its presence in certain gestures or facial expressions may be too subtle for many trainees.

SUMMARY

Four particularly effective procedures for skills training—modeling, role playing, performance feedback, and transfer of training and maintenance—have been examined in detail. The nature of each procedure, the techniques that maximize their impact, a sample of the wide variety of learning targets to which each has been applied successfully, and samples of supporting research have been presented. Yet, in discussing each procedure, enthusiasm was lessened by one or more cautionary notes. For example, although modeling does indeed result in the learning of new behaviors, without sufficient practice, old behaviors clearly tend to recur. Practice, or role playing, is also an important aid in new learning, but one must practice correct behaviors, and without prior modeling or similar demonstration, the trainee's performance is improved very little over its initial level. Given both modeling and role playing, the newly learned behaviors have greater likelihood of persisting but will not do so unless the trainee sees that the use of these behaviors will be personally rewarding. This problem highlights the crucial necessity of reinforcement through performance feedback; however, even the availability of reinforcement is frequently insufficient for effective human learning. The behaviors to be reinforced must be enacted by the trainee correctly and with sufficient frequency that adequate opportunity for reinforcement occurs. Without such procedures, the new behaviors, even if reinforced, may occur too seldom for stable learning to take place. Thus, procedures such as modeling and role playing can lead to such sufficient frequency of correct enactment. Combining these three procedures yields a much more effective and applicable approach to skills training. Yet, a truly effective approach to learning must also demonstrate such learning beyond the training setting and must prove to be powerful, useful, and reliably enduring in the learner's real-life settings. This latter concern has prompted the inclusion of, and emphasis on, techniques for enhancing transfer of training and maintenance. The following chapter describes and illustrates these specific Structured Learning techniques and procedures as they are implemented within a mental health context.

Chapter 3

Structured Learning: Implementation Procedures

The reader has been introduced to the likely recipients of social skills training: psychiatric patients in outpatient clinics, community residences, hospitals, and nursing homes. Although these individuals may have traveled via different routes to these various settings, and may carry a range of psychiatric diagnoses, all can be described as deficient in a range of social skills that interferes with their abilities to function effectively in their daily lives. The reader has also learned about the background and development of a particular approach to social skills training known as Structured Learning. It is now time to weave the two together and show how Structured Learning is actually implemented with this psychiatric population.

This chapter deals with the procedures used in organizing and conducting a Structured Learning group. First, the overall criteria for developing Structured Learning groups are discussed. Next, the selection of appropriate participants for the groups is explained, along with the types of assessment procedures that are typically used. The selection, orientation, and training of group leaders are described. Finally, an actual group is described and outlined for group leaders to use as a model for implementing their own Structured Learning groups.

OVERALL CRITERIA

In the selection of appropriate participants for Structured Learning groups it is important for trainers to keep two principles in mind: (1) try to select participants who share similar skill deficiencies, so that the skill-training efforts will have immediate relevance for their lives, and (2) try to work within naturally occurring groups or units—clinic, residence, ward—so that the logistics of conducting a group can be as painless as possible and transfer from training setting to real-life contexts can be encouraged. What is absent from these basic principles is any mention of selection or grouping according to formal diagnoses. Whereas it may be true that many people who are diagnosed as schizophrenic, for example, may also be described as deficient in a variety of social skills, such deficiencies may also be found in people who are depressed or alcoholic or otherwise diagnosed. That the person him- or herself as well as those in the person's environment are able to recognize the skill deficit is far more important than psychiatric diagnosis. As will be discussed shortly, assessment for social skills training is based largely on self- and others' perceptions of appropriateness of behaviors in interpersonal situations rather than on more formal psychological or psychiatric evaluations. This type of assessment is also linked more closely to the individual's motivation for participation in training—if the person sees a deficit, then he or she is more likely to wish to do something about it.

SELECTION AND GROUPING

Trainees in Structured Learning groups are selected primarily in terms of their proficiencies or deficiencies in the skills that are to be addressed (and discussed in detail in chapter 4). These skills are defined in understandable language so that the trainee can appreciate the skill's meaning and relevance. Likewise, others who have the opportunity to interact with the person—family, peers, and paraprofessional and professional staff—can contribute to the selection and assessment process.

Structured Learning is primarily a psychoeducational group procedure that requires the trainee to be able to attend to the material being discussed and to participate actively, or at least not disrupt the on-going process. Thus, trainees who are unable to pay attention for a minimal amount of time (as little as 15 minutes) should not be included in the training. Likewise, those persons who absolutely refuse to cooperate, presumably because they see no relevance of the Structured Learning group to their lives, should be excluded until their motivation to participate can be enhanced. Some techniques for increasing appropriate participation will be discussed in chapter 5. Some individual problems of distractability attributable to psychotic processes, anxiety, or depression can be helped greatly with psychiatric medication, so that the person can pay attention to the immediate group experience.

Prospective Structured Learning group members are usually nominated by staff in the facilities in which they are seen. Thus, staff should be made aware of the availability of the Structured Learning group and be provided with some general idea as to what it will involve and who might be appropriate for inclusion. Those staff members who will be serving as the Structured Learning trainers are likely to be responsible for selecting and inviting participants to join Structured Learning groups. For purposes of initial selection, Structured Learning groups may be described in general terms (e.g., "a social skills training group" or "a positive skill-building group"), which should allow for initial nomination by staff or self-selection by potential trainees. As the specific focus of the group becomes more clearly articulated, particular skills or groups of skills can be presented (e.g., "basic conversational skills" or "aggression management skills"). Potential members' skill proficiencies may be observed and evaluated naturalistically. Using the Structured Learning Skill Questionnaire in the appendix, staff may evaluate potential participants in terms of behaviors they have observed in a range of settings (clinic, ward, or community residence). However, it should be kept in mind that skill proficiencies or deficiencies tend to be situation-specific: the person may demonstrate good conversational skills in the day room, for example, but do very poorly when attempting to talk with a clerk in a store. Thus, if the Skill Questionnaire is used in selecting group members, the situations in which the person is more or less proficient or deficient should be specified.

The client may also be interviewed and asked directly about perceived skill deficiencies or proficiencies. Such interviews can also serve as a way of introducing Structured Learning and inviting and motivating the person to participate. In addition to the self-reports elicited during these interviews, behaviors in the interview situations can also be observed and evaluated. Indeed, an interview may serve as an assessment situation in which a range of interpersonal behaviors may be observed and evaluated. Does the person establish and maintain eye contact? Does he or she appear to be listening? Does he or she ask appropriate questions? These types of behaviors, or others more directly linked to those defined on the Skill Questionnaire, may be incorporated into an interview situation. The interviewer may even wish to engage the potential group member in a role-play situation to assess the person's particular skill use, as well as his or her ability to role play. By describing a social interaction and inviting the person to participate, a specific sample of behavior may be obtained (e.g., "Let's pretend I'm a clerk at Sears, and you want to return a shirt that you bought there"). Participants themselves may also complete the Skill Questionnaire, which may be a good indicator of motivation to participate. Sometimes this type of questionnaire can help some individuals to express their felt needs, even if their perceptions differ markedly from those of people who might observe and evaluate them. Indeed, these discrepancies constitute valuable information about how the individual might be approached in the group in order to maximize motivation.

A final method of selection is based on the longstanding principle that "the best predictor of behavior is behavior." That is, if one wishes to predict how well a particular person or a group of people will do in a Structured Learning group, one may constitute a short-term, trial group. If the client or mix of clients do well in a time-limited group experience, then the likelihood of their performing appropriately in a longer series of such meetings is that much greater. Such trial groups may be as short as a single session. In addition to providing an excellent sample of potential trainees' behaviors in a Structured Learning group, trial groups can serve as potent motivators for reticent trainees and can acquaint new group members with Structured Learning procedures.

STRUCTURED LEARNING TRAINERS

Structured Learning groups are psychoeducational, behavioral, action-oriented endeavors aimed at teaching important interpersonal skills to persons deficient in such skills. As discussed in chapter 2, the major goal is to not only help people acquire necessary skills, but to use these skills in their daily lives. Trainers play an essential role in this process and must be effective communicators and teachers. They also must be very familiar with the interpersonal worlds of their clients. They must "speak the language" of their group members, both literally and figuratively, and be attuned to the details and subtleties of their references to their environments. The formal degrees and job titles of trainers appear to be less important than other characteristics described next; trainers may be counselors, social workers, psychologists, psychiatrists, therapy aides, nurses, or residence staff.

Structured Learning procedures are active, involving modeling, role playing, and feedback. In order to permit these activities to proceed, two trainers are generally needed. They must enact the modeling displays, "set the stage," serve as co-actors in role plays at times, direct the role playing, elicit feedback, assign homework, and manage the progress and direction of the group, as well as deal with occasional problematic behaviors within the group. Two types of skills are desirable for Structured Learning trainers to have. The first type is helpful for anyone who leads any kind of group and may be referred to as general leadership skills. These consist of such qualities or skills as empathy, warmth, enthusiasm, spontaneity, trustworthiness, listening ability, ability to provide norms and structure, and ability to provide reinforcement. In addition, there are trainer skills that are more specific to Structured Learning groups. These skills include:

1. Knowledge of Structured Learning background and procedures
2. Knowledge of basic behavioral principles
3. Ability to present material in concrete terms
4. Ability to orient staff and group members about Structured Learning
5. Ability to plan and present modeling displays
6. Ability to lead role plays
7. Ability to elicit and provide corrective feedback
8. Ability to utilize homework assignments and other transfer enhancers
9. Ability to manage problematic behaviors that may occur in a Structured Learning group.

The best way to teach Structured Learning procedures to new trainers is by using Structured Learning procedures. In addition to familiarizing new group leaders with Structured Learning via written and didactic materials, they are asked to participate in a role-played Structured Learning group, with two group leaders. Trainers-in-training assume the identities or characteristics of clients with whom they will likely be dealing. They are instructed to become these characters in as many ways as possible and to present the kinds of concerns that their future group members are likely to present. Once a group of these role-played clients is constituted, the trainers go through a typical group. After their participation as clients, the trainers-in-training take turns co-leading the role-played group and receive corrective feedback on their performances. They then go out and develop their own Structured Learning groups, meeting periodically, when possible, for continued exchange of ideas, supervision, feedback, and support. Thus, the components of modeling, role playing, corrective feedback, and transfer of training and maintenance are built into the training of Structured Learning trainers.

CONDUCTING STRUCTURED LEARNING GROUPS

Structured Learning group members are selected primarily because they share common skills deficits and they share common interpersonal worlds. This latter element is particularly important in terms of the transfer enhancement principle of identical elements. This principle states that the more alike the training environment is to the real-life environment, the more likely it will be that what is learned will be applied effectively in the real-life setting. The interpersonal aspects of these environments are critically important, but physical characteristics are also important. By necessity, training usually takes place in a somewhat "unnatural" setting—a ward, classroom, day room, or clinic. However, even these unnatural settings can be made to resemble natural settings in as many ways as possible. Thus, it is useful to have available furnishings and props to help transform training settings into real-life settings. Desks, easy chairs, telephones, and the like are some of the things that can help in these transformations. For example, if a group member is preparing for a conversation with his boss who usually sits behind a desk, he should not only select a co-actor who resembles his boss in some ways, but also should have a desk (or a table) for his boss to sit behind. If another client is preparing for a conversation with her mother that will take place in her mother's living room on the couch, then she and her co-actor should rehearse on a couch. Creativity and imagination in transforming the training setting not only increases the likelihood of transfer, but also is likely to increase involvement and motivation. If a group member is planning to talk with a clerk who stands behind the counter in a store, then a table can become the counter with minimal effort.

Structured Learning groups are psychoeducational endeavors whose goals are the acquisition and transfer of important interpersonal skills. They are conducted within a variety of settings and must accommodate to the norms, atmospheres, characteristics, and schedules of those settings. Whereas it is desirable to hold Structured Learning groups twice a week for 45 minutes to 1 hour for each group, in some settings only a single meeting a week is possible. In a community residence, a Structured Learning group (perhaps referred to as a "Socialization Group") may meet three evenings a week after supper in the living room. In a more structured, educational setting, a "Social Skills Class" may meet three times a week for a "semester." The main concern is that enough time is allowed for modeling, role playing, and feedback during the sessions, and for skill practice outside of the group between sessions. In some settings, groups are time limited; other settings are built around open-ended activities.

Characteristics of trainees must also be considered in making scheduling determinations. Although 45 minutes to 1 hour is a typical and desirable session length, some highly distractable trainees may be able to tolerate only a 15 or 20 minute group experience. If this is the case, then more frequent meetings should be held. The usual size of Structured Learning groups is four to eight trainees plus two trainers. Fewer than four trainees limits the opportunities for relevant role plays;

greater than eight or nine trainees usually means less involvement of each participant at each session, with some losing interest.

Getting Started

The first session of a new Structured Learning group is critical in arousing participant interest and motivation to become actively involved and to continue in the group. Although it is necessary to acquaint group members with group norms, rules, and procedures, too much structuring at this stage is to be discouraged. Rather, the trainers try to establish a comfortable, nonthreatening atmosphere while moving quickly through preliminaries. Getting started may consist of having the trainers introduce themselves and inviting group members to introduce and tell a little about themselves. Trainers then provide a brief overview of Structured Learning, in nontechnical language, attempting to illustrate ways in which it may prove helpful to members:

> "We'll be teaching skills that should be helpful in getting along more comfortably with people. For example, we might try to help you to talk to your boss without losing your temper; we might want to work on helping you to be able to ask a family member for some assistance at home."

A description of Structured Learning procedures might consist of:

> "We'll be working on one skill at a time. First, we'll show you some examples of how you can use that skill. Then, you'll each have a turn to try the skill in situations that might come up in your lives. Then, we'll tell you how well you used the skill. Finally, you'll have a chance to practice it in real life."

After these brief introductory comments by the trainers, along with statements about procedural rules ("The group will meet every Monday and Thursday at this time. It's very important that you come to every session."), trainers quickly introduce a skill and provide a modeling display. The first skill chosen should be relevant to the majority of members and should be simple enough so that all are likely be successful in their initial attempts.

> "The first skill we're going to cover is the skill of starting a conversation. We all have to start conversations every day, and sometimes it's not easy."

The concept of breaking skills down into their behavioral steps is presented at the outset:

> "When we start a conversation, we do so by following these four steps that are written on the board. First, you greet the other person. Second, you make small talk. Third, you decide if the other person is listening. Finally, you bring up the main topic. If you've gone through the steps correctly, then you've done the skill."

Modeling

The modeling displays illustrate effective skill use. Thus, the displays must be such that group members can identify with them in terms of situation, language, and setting. During each Structured Learning session only one skill should be modeled at a time, although at least two examples, or vignettes, should be presented. This is done so that the skill concept is shown to be generalizable across situations. As such, the content of each modeling vignette should be quite different from the preceding one. The situations depicted in the modeling displays should be familiar to the lives of group members. All modeling displays should portray positive and realistic outcomes, with a great deal of reinforcement for the main actor for having performed the skill correctly. Usually, the two trainers will present the modeling displays live. However, audio- and videotaped modeling displays have also been used successfully. Sometimes, group members can be involved in the modeling, but this is seldom done in early sessions. (A listing of the Structured Learning skills, detailed instructions for developing modeling displays, and suggestions for situations to be modeled are presented in chapter 4.) A modeling display might consist of the following:

> "We're going to show you a few examples of how to start a conversation by following the steps that are written on the board. In the first example, I'm going to pretend to start a conversation with a sales clerk in a store. Ms. Johnson is going to take the role of the clerk, and she'll be standing behind a counter. Let's pretend that this table is the sales counter. I want to talk to the salesperson about some shirts that were advertised in the paper. The first step says to greet the other person: 'Good morning, miss.' 'Good morning. How can I help you?' The next step says to make small talk. 'I'm sure glad it's not as crowded today as it was last week.' 'Yes, it was crowded last week, our yearly sale, you know.' The third step tells you to decide if the other person is listening. This is one that you do in your head, but I'll say it out loud so that you can tell what I'm thinking. 'She seems to be listening because she's nodding and looking at me.' Finally, the fourth step tells you to bring up the main topic. 'Miss, I saw some sport shirts advertised in the newspaper that were supposed to be on sale. Can you tell me where they are?'"

Role Playing

Once the group members have observed the modeling displays, trainers attempt to stimulate a discussion of what has been seen. The focus of the discussion is the situations portrayed and how those situations remind members of times in their own lives when they have had to use the skill and, most important, of times when they might have to use the skill again. Trainers stay attuned to identifying problematic aspects of present and future skill use, thus developing content for the first role play.

Trainers may encourage a group member who has commented on the modeling to describe a time in the foreseeable future when use of the skill being discussed would be helpful. Once identified, the group member (now identified as the main actor) is encouraged to describe the situation in which he or she might use the skill and to choose someone in the group who resembles the other primary person (the co-actor) with whom he or she will role play. The co-actor is asked to take on the role of the real-life other person in as many ways as possible, including physical appearance, manner of speech, and mood. The setting in which the interaction is likely to take place is also described in detail by the main actor, and the trainers attempt to transform the training room, through the use of furniture, props, and imagination, so that it begins to approximate the real-life environment.

Having set the stage, the trainers then review the skill steps with the main actor and may rehearse part of the role play before the full enactment. The chalkboard is positioned so that the main actor and the other group members are able to read the behavioral steps that have been written on it. Before beginning the role play, all participants are reminded of their responsibilities: the main actor is told to follow the behavioral steps; the co-actor is told to respond to the main actor in ways that seem appropriate; the other group members are urged to watch for the portrayal of the behavioral steps. To make the task even more concrete for certain populations, particular group members may be given the task of watching for particular steps as they are enacted. The observers are also told to look for qualitative aspects of the performance, such as eye contact, tone of voice, verbal content, and overall effectiveness. During the role play, one trainer is available as a coach or stage director. The other trainer may choose to sit with the other group members in order to encourage attentiveness and appropriate feedback. The following is an example of a role play:

Trainer 1:   Lamar, you mentioned that the example we just showed you reminded you that you wanted to talk to your supervisor about giving you some more responsibilities at work. Is that something you would like to practice here?

Lamar: I guess I better. I'll never get a raise unless I'm given more duties.

Trainer 1:   OK. Good. Let's figure out what you're going to say and how you're going to say it. What's your supervisor's name?

Lamar: Mr. Martinez.

Trainer 2:   What's Mr. Martinez like? What does he look like? How does he act?

Lamar: Well, he's a big man, with a loud voice. He's on the phone alot.

Trainer 2:   Who in the group reminds you of Mr. Martinez?

Lamar: I guess Bill comes closest. He's kinda big and has a big voice.

Trainer 2:   OK. Bill, will you come up and take the part of Mr. Martinez? Good.

Trainer 1:   Let's try to get some more information. Where would be the best time and place to talk to Mr. Martinez?

Lamar: He's always at his desk, which is at the back of the file room, and he's always on the phone.

Trainer 1:   And the best time?

Lamar: Well, he's always busy, but I guess that the first thing in the morning would be best. Before the phone starts ringing. When he's drinking his coffee.

Trainer 2:   OK. Let's pretend that this table is Mr. Martinez' desk. Bill, let's have you sit behind the desk. And we have a phone. Anything else? Oh, a coffee cup. What else would help make Bill seem like Mr. Martinez? How should he talk? What's his mood likely to be?

Lamar: He always talks loud, and fast. He's not really angry, but he seems that way. You know, like "whatta you want?" in a loud voice.

Trainer 2:   OK., Bill, do you have some idea of what Mr. Martinez is like?

Bill: Yeah, I know a guy like that. But what should I say?

Trainer 1:   You respond to what Lamar says. We'll help you out if you get stuck. If Lamar does a good job, make sure you go along with him.

Trainer 2:   Lamar, it's the first thing in the morning, and Mr. Martinez is sitting behind his desk, drinking coffee. And you're going to start a conversation with him about taking on more responsibilities. And you're going to do it by following these steps that are written on the board. OK. Step one says, "Greet the other person." How will you greet him?

Lamar: That's easy. I'll say, "Good morning."

Trainer 2:   And step two: "Make small talk." You know, like talking about the weather.

Lamar: He's a big sports fan. I'll ask him if he watched the game last night.

Trainer 2:   Good. And step three; that's the one that you do in your head. But I'd like you to say it out loud, so that everyone can tell what you are thinking. "Decide if the other person is listening." How will you know if he's listening?

Lamar: If he's listening he'll look up; he won't be on the phone.

Trainer 2:   Good. And the fourth step: "Bring up the main topic." What is the main topic you want to talk to him about?

Lamar: His giving me more work duties.

Trainer 2:   OK. What would be a good thing to say to him?

Lamar: Well, I'll tell him that I've been there 6 months and I get all my work done on time, and I don't make mistakes, and I can do more.

Trainer 1:   Very good. OK. We're ready to go. Lamar, you're going to go through the steps that are on the board in front; Bill, you're going to pretend to be Mr. Martinez and respond to what Lamar says to you. The rest of the group will be watching to see if you follow the steps and to see how well you do. Keisha, will you watch for step one? Charles, how about step two? Tina, step three is the one in which he's thinking out loud. Will you look for that one? And step four, the main topic; Stan, will you pay special attention to that one. And the rest of us will watch the whole thing. OK. Let's begin.

Lamar: Good morning, Mr. Martinez.

Bill: Morning, Lamar.

Lamar: Did you happen to see the game last night on TV?

Bill: Yeah, it was a close one.

Lamar: Well, he's looking at me, and he's not on the phone. I guess he's listening.

Lamar: Mr. Martinez. There's something I wanted to talk to you about. I've been working here 6 months, and I always get my work done on time, and I don't make many mistakes. I was wondering . . . could you give me some more duties? I can handle them.

Bill: Like what?

Lamar: Like data entry or supplies.

Bill: I don't see why not. You're a good worker.

Feedback

Following the completion of each role play, a brief feedback period ensues. The purposes of this feedback are to provide the main actor with both constructive criticism on how well he or she did in enacting the skill and to stimulate motivation to actually attempt the skill in real life. Thus, the trainers must be careful to ensure that the feedback is positive and is directed toward future implementation. It is also important that the feedback is framed in concrete, behavioral terms rather than global, evaluative generalities.

The usual sequence for the feedback is to first ask the co-actor how he or she felt the main actor performed in interacting with him or her:

> "Bill, how well do you feel that Lamar did in starting a conversation with you? What did he do well? What might he improve?"

After the co-actor has provided initial reactions, the group members are asked for their responses. Because some of them may have been given particular aspects of the enactment to look for, they may be asked about those particular behaviors as a way to concretizing the feedback:

> OK. Let's get some feedback for Lamar from the rest of the group. Let's begin with step one. Keisha, you had step one. Did Lamar greet Mr. Martinez? What did he say? Was there anything he could have done to make it even better?
>
> Who had the second step, the one about small talk? What else could he have said?
>
> Step three, "Decide if the other person is listening." How did Lamar decide?
>
> And step four, Stan, did he open the main topic? How else might he have done it?
>
> Any other specific suggestions or comments from the group? What about eye contact? How was his tone of voice?

After obtaining feedback from group members, the trainers can add their comments. Because these comments are likely to carry considerable weight, trainers should refrain from giving them too early, for fear of limiting further discussion. Trainers must make particular efforts to follow any negative comment with constructive suggestions on how the behavior might be improved. If a role play is so deficient that there is very little to reinforce, then the trainers should instruct the main actor to try again and should reinforce approximations of the desired behaviors. Trainers should also vary the content of the feedback sessions so that they do not become rote and uninformative:

> "What I thought was particularly good was the way you waited until Mr. Martinez stopped talking on the phone before you began speaking. That's

very important to do. You might want to try to use a little more small talk next time as well. Otherwise, I thought you did a very good job. Ms. Johnson, any other feedback or suggestions for Lamar?"

Finally, the main actor is given an opportunity to comment on his or her performance. If the trainers have been sufficiently directive in their elicitation of feedback from group members, then the main actor's reactions should be embellishments on what has been said already:

Trainer 1:   Lamar, how do you feel you did in starting a conversation with Mr. Martinez?

Lamar: I guess it went pretty well. I was a little nervous.

Trainer 1:   I'll bet that the next time you practice it you won't be quite so nervous. Is there anything that you think you should do differently to make it even better?

Lamar: I don' know. Maybe some more small talk, like you said.

It is important to provide feedback and reinforcement to the co-actor and the group members as well, because appropriate feedback is an integral part of the Structured Learning procedure and must also be taught and encouraged.

Trainer 2:   I wanted to compliment the group members for your comments, which I thought were very helpful. Those of you who were watching for the steps really seemed like you were paying close attention. And Bill, you were very convincing as Mr. Martinez."

Transfer of Training and Maintenance

Given enough training, repetition, encouragement, and group support, most trainees will learn and demonstrate the skills and behaviors taught in Structured Learning groups while they are involved in the groups. However, the transfer of these skills from the training setting to the real-life setting is often more difficult to accomplish. Unless explicit attention is paid to the issue of transfer of training and maintenance, little is likely to become incorporated into clients' behavioral repertoires or to make much positive impact on their lives.

The assignment of homework is the most familiar vehicle for effecting the transfer of newly learned skills. With the use of homework assignments, group members are instructed explicitly to practice the skill that has been role played in the group in a predetermined situation outside of the group. Using the Homework Practice Form #1 (see Figure 1) as the structure, group members who have successfully role played a skill in the group are asked to specify when, where, and with whom they plan to use the skill before the next meeting. They are also asked to write down the steps they plan to follow. After trying the skill in real life, and prior to the next group meeting, they are asked to record and evaluate how well they did in using the skill, what steps were actually followed, how they would rate their performance, and what the next homework assignment should be.

The first part of subsequent group sessions is devoted to reviewing the homework assignments from the previous group session. Participants are provided with social reinforcement for attempts and approximations of successful skill use. If the person attempted the

FIGURE 1.

Homework Practice Form #1

Name _____ Date _____

Group Leaders: _____

FILL IN DURING CLASS

1. What skill will you use?

2. Write in the steps for the skill.

_____

_____

_____

_____

_____

3. Where will you try the skill?

4. With whom will you try the skill?

5. When will you try the skill?

FILL IN AFTER DOING YOUR HOMEWORK

1. What happened when you did your homework?

2. Which steps did you really follow?

3. How good a job did you do?

    Excellent _____ Good _____ Fair _____ Poor _____

4. Can you think of any other homework using this skill?

homework but reports that it went very poorly, then the failure may serve as the basis for a re-role play. Those who do not attempt their homework assignments are urged to do so, emphasizing the critical importance of real-life practice. If homework is not a realistic expectation with particular group members, they can be asked to do their practice right in the group (e.g., try starting a conversation with the group leader). Returning to the illustration, the following feedback might be offered:

Trainer: Lamar, at the end of the last group meeting you agreed that you were ready to actually start a conversation with Mr. Martinez. Why don't we begin by you telling the rest of the group about your homework attempt.

Lamar: Well, I tried it. It's all written down, here on this paper.

Trainer: OK. Let's have a look. You listed the skill and the steps. Good. And you were planning to try it on Thursday morning, at work, with Mr. Martinez. What happened?

Lamar: It went OK, I guess. I mean, I went through it pretty much like we practiced it here last time. Only . . .

Trainer: Yes?

Lamar: Well, I went through all the steps, but when I got to the last one, the phone started ringing, so I never got to ask him about my taking on more duties.

Trainer: What did he say?

Lamar: He said that he couldn't talk now, "Catch me some other time."

Keisha: You did good, Lamar. Ask him again.

Trainer: How do you think you did?

Lamar: Fair. I should have talked faster.

Trainer: It sounds like you did pretty well, but maybe you just needed a little more time. How would you feel about trying it again? What would you do differently?

Lamar: I guess I should try to catch him a little earlier. Maybe on Tuesday.

Trainer: You're off to a real good start. You covered all of the steps. Just the timing needs to be worked on. How about if we make that your next homework assignment. How do you feel about that? Do you think you need some more practice here?

Lamar: No, I'm OK.

Trainer: Any other comments or suggestions for Lamar? Good job!

Self Reward and External Reward

It is assumed in this and in other psychoeducational approaches to skills training that for newly learned or relearned behaviors to be maintained they must be reinforced in real-life settings. However, all too often the process stops there, assuming or hoping that sufficient naturalistic reinforcement will be forthcoming. Rather than leaving this critical aspect of transfer of training to chance, Structured Learning attempts to build in some specific procedures to ensure that rewards will be available outside of the training room. One technique is to give the client the capability of providing self-rewards. That is, the client is taught basic principles of self-reinforcement and is instructed to say and do self-rewarding things after practicing a newly acquired skill well. The Homework Practice Form #2 (see Figure 2) may be useful in helping clients conceptualize and plan for these rewards. In addition to asking clients to identify the what, when, and with whom of anticipated skill use, they are asked to plan their self-reward activities, trying to tailor the magnitude of the reward to the quality of the performance. A particular effort is made to help participants differentiate between process and outcome; that is, they are taught that they may be worthy of self-reward if they performed the skill well, even if the desired effect was not obtained. Further, group members are instructed on how to select appropriate

FIGURE 2.

Homework Practice Form #2

Name _____   Date _____

Group Leaders: _____

FILL IN DURING CLASS

  1. What skill will you use?

  2. Write in the steps for the skill.

_____

_____

_____

_____

3. Where will you try the skill?

4. With whom will you try the skill?

5. When will you try the skill?

6. If you do an excellent job, how will you reward yourself?

_____

_____

_____

7. If you do a good job, how will you reward yourself?

_____

_____

_____

8. If you do a fair job, how will you reward yourself?

_____

_____

_____

_____

FILL IN AFTER DOING YOUR HOMEWORK

1. What happened when you did your homework?

2. Which steps did you really follow?

3. How good a job did you do?

   Excellent _____ Good _____ Fair _____ Poor _____

4. How did you reward yourself?

_____

_____

5. What do you think should be your next homework assignment?

rewards—such rewards must indeed be special and not something that is said or done routinely. Once the principles of self-reward are explained, discussed, and implemented, they can be carried out fairly independently, without requiring much group time.

Trainer: Lamar, you've been doing homework assignments for a couple of weeks now on the skill of starting a conversation. You seem to be doing pretty well, and I know that it's something that you want to keep working on.

Lamar: Yeah, I know if I don't force myself, I'll just slip into the woodwork again.

Trainer: One of the ways that we use to help people to keep working on important skills is learning how to reward themselves (distributes copies of Homework Practice Form #2). As you can see, the first part of the form looks pretty much like the homework form you've been using. But if you look at the middle of the sheet, you'll see that there are a few questions about "how will you reward yourself." See them?

Lamar: Yeah.

Trainer: Let me tell you a little about this. One thing that really helps motivation is for you to say encouraging things to yourself and do something nice for yourself after you've worked on something that's important to you. It makes you feel good when other people tell you that you've done a good job, but other people aren't always there, and they don't always tell you those things.

Charles: You can say that again!

Trainer: That's why we try to teach you to reward yourself. An important thing about these rewards is that they're a little special: you save them for special accomplishments. And the other thing to remember is that you are rewarding yourself for doing what you had planned, even if the other person doesn't always respond the way you hoped that he would. I think it will be clearer if we use an example. Lamar, since you're ready to start on the Homework Practice Form #2, let's use your situation, if that's OK.

Lamar: Sure.

Trainer: Let's look at the form. The first couple of questions are the same as before: what skill and what steps. You're still working on the skill of starting a conversation, so you can write that in. And the steps are the same, so copy those. The next questions ask where, when, and with whom you plan to use the skill.

Lamar: Yeah, I think I should try to talk to Mrs. Henry, the Personnel Manager. Mr. Martinez told me that if I ever wanted to get ahead, I needed to start bidding on new jobs.

Trainer: Good idea. When do you think you'll try to talk with her? And where?

Lamar: It's gotta be in her office. I'll have to make an appointment. Next week, sometime. Maybe Mr. Martinez will let me go up to Personnel one afternoon next week, when things slow down in the file room. I'd better check with him and then make an appointment.

Trainer: Right. OK, put that information under those questions on the form. Now, here's the part about rewarding yourself. "If you do an excellent job, how will you reward yourself?" What we mean is, what should you say to yourself, and what should you do for yourself if you really do a good job in using the skill. Remember, it's not necessary for you to be offered a new job, because that may not be possible. What's important here is if you used the skill really well.

Lamar: I think I understand what you mean. Well, I could say to myself, "I really did good. I should be proud of myself."

Trainer: That's the idea. And what about doing something special for yourself, something out of the ordinary?

Lamar: You mean like buying something? Going somewhere? Well, if I really did a great job, maybe I could call my brother up and talk for a while. I don't call him very often because he lives in Yorktown and it costs a dollar for 3 minutes. But that's not too bad. I like talking to him.

Trainer: You've got the idea. And what about if you did a fair job? How would you reward yourself? What could you say?

The effort devoted to explaining self-reward principles usually does not have to be repeated in subsequent group sessions. Rather, individuals who are working on continuing skill practice using self-reward can arrange to meet briefly with trainers before or after group meetings to keep them abreast of their progress. Indeed, this shift toward independent practice and monitoring serves to highlight and reinforce the notion of self-reward.

Some group members may not be capable of self-reward initially, or even over an extended period of time. Rather, some may require that external rewards be provided in their environments in order for their newly learned behaviors to be utilized outside of the group. This is best done via social reinforcement from significant people in their real-life environments outside of the training room. In a day treatment center or a community residence, for example, those staff members who are not involved directly as trainers can be informed as to the goals and procedures of Structured Learning. It is often helpful to hold an orientation meeting for this purpose. Staff may then be asked to be particularly attentive to certain behaviors or skills, so that they might reinforce trainees' attempts to practice these skills.

Trainer: Joyce, you know Charles, who attends our Tuesday Social Skills group, don't you?

Joyce: Oh, you mean the tall, quiet man. Yeah, I know him, but he usually avoids looking at me when he comes in, and he seldom talks.

Trainer: That's the one. Well, he's been working on the skill of asking for help, so sometime this week he may ask you to help him with something. We'd appreciate it if you'd let him know that he did it well, if he does OK, that is.

Joyce: No problem.

With some clients who may be quite limited intellectually or more severely impaired psychiatrically, external, tangible rewards may be implemented within the context of the Structured Learning group. The psychoeducational nature of Structured Learning makes it quite compatible with token economies and other similar systems, whereby appropriate behaviors are rewarded immediately with points or tokens. These tangible reinforcers can be exchanged for desirable activities (e.g., trips, free time) or commodities (e.g., candy, sodas). The "menu" for earning and spending points or tokens can be written on the chalkboard, and reviewed for those who may have difficulty reading:

Role playing = 5 points
Giving feedback = 3 points
Doing homework = 5 points
Asking questions = 1 point

Soda = 25 points
Donut = 25 points
Movie = 40 points
Crafts projects = 40–80 points

SUMMARY

In this chapter, we have detailed the Structured Learning procedures. We encouraged new trainers to use the Structured Learning method for their own training in becoming group leaders. Many examples of Structured Learning procedures in use were provided to assist new leaders in implementing the techniques described.

Chapter 4

Structured Learning Skills

The beginning of this chapter presents a menu of social skills which we have found useful to teach to clients. It is not an exhaustive list by any means. As you work with these skills, and as you get to know your clients, you will surely find that we have left out some skills which you consider critical for your group. You will see that you can add your own skills fairly simply, by taking time to come up with steps, try them out, and see how your clients respond. Some of the skills and steps for those skills which we have developed have a long and solid research history. Others have been developed through our own clinical experience. So do join us in that effort. In developing your own steps for skills you wish to add, we recommend that trainers use the following guiding principles:

1. Use three to five steps for each skill.
2. Use nontechnical language that is easily understood by your client population.
3. Make each step clear and distinct.
4. Make each step behaviorally specific, eliminating any extraneous details.
5. Phrase steps positively (e.g., "Do this" rather than "Don't do this").

Readers will notice immediately that the subgroup of skills entitled "Skills for dealing with feelings" includes a short list of only four skills. Actually, the number of skills in this section could have been endless and could have included the expression of many different feelings, i.e. , expressing anger, expressing affection, expressing sorrow, and so on. Rather than do it this way, we have chosen to include the skill of expressing your feelings. Trainers can then tailor the actual content of the session to the particular skills on which clients need to work.

Each skill in this chapter has a list of steps, trainer notes, suggested content for modeling displays, and comments. The steps are the backbone of the skill. They are what is actually modeled by the trainers and role played by the clients. The trainer notes are based on our own observations about how to engage clients in discussing the skill and making it relevant to their lives.

The suggested content for modeling displays gives trainers a range of ideas for developing their own displays. Trainers will find that some of this content is useful, whereas other aspects are not at all relevant to their clientele. Again, we invite you to join us in developing displays that are most relevant for your population.

SKILL LIST

Skill Group: Beginning Social Skills

1. Starting a conversation
2. Listening
3. Ending a conversation
4. Asking for help
5. Following instructions
6. Giving a compliment
7. Saying "thank you"
8. Apologizing

Skill Group: Skills for Dealing with Feelings

9. Expressing your feelings
10. Understanding the feelings of others
11. Preparing for a stressful conversation
12. Reacting to failure

Skill Group: Assertiveness Skills

13. Standing up for your rights
14. Helping others
15. Giving instructions
16. Making a complaint
17. Answering a complaint
18. Negotiation
19. Self-control
20. Persuasion
21. Responding to persuasion
22. Dealing with group pressure

Skill Group: Problem-solving Skills

23. Setting priorities
24. Making decisions
25. Setting a goal
26. Concentrating on a task
27. Rewarding yourself

GROUP: Beginning Social Skills
SKILL 1: Starting a conversation

Steps	Trainer Notes
1. Greet the other person.	Choose the right time and place, say hello, shake hands.
2. Make small talk.	
3. Decide if the other person wants to talk with you.	Observe body language, eye contact.
4. Bring up the main topic.	Use this step only when this skill is used as a lead-in to a more serious conversation.

Suggested Content for Modeling Displays

A. Neighborhood: You introduce yourself to a next door neighbor.

B. Home: You speak up at the dinner table.

C. Clinic/hospital: You chat with someone in the office before a doctor's appointment.

Comments

We have found that this is one of the best skills to teach in the first session with a new group of trainees. This skill puts considerable emphasis on reading the reactions of others (Step 3). We encourage trainees to practice this step many times, with the goal of sensitizing them to noticing whether others are attending and/or interested in what they are discussing.

Many of the steps which make up the skills described in this chapter are thinking steps. Step 3 falls into this category. We recommend that when you model or role play such steps, trainers and trainees should enact their thinking processes out loud. If trainees have difficulty with this concept, trainers can use a question-answer format. In Step 3, the trainer might ask: "Can you tell whether _____ wants to talk with you? How can you tell?"

GROUP: Beginning Social Skills
SKILL 2: Listening

Steps	Trainer Notes
1. Look at the person who is talking.	Establish eye contact.
2. Think about what is being said.	Use body language to show that you are paying attention (nod head, sit forward in chair).
3. Wait your turn to talk.	Look for cues that the other person is finished talking.
4. Say what you want to say.	Stay on the topic, ask questions, express feelings, express ideas.

Suggested Content for Modeling Displays

A. Neighborhood: You are listening to someone explain how to get to the laundromat.

B. Home: Your roommate has a serious problem.

C. Clinic/hospital: The nurse is explaining how to take your medication.

Comments

All of the beginning social skills are basic to the functioning of the group. We recommend that trainers work with trainees on these basic social skills until a core of group members has a reasonable grasp of these skills. Trainers will find that many in-group situations can be used as examples of appropriate beginning social skills. These can then be used as modeling displays.

Trainers are reminded that Step 2 and Step 3 are "think out loud" steps. Special attention should be paid to these in modeling and role playing.

GROUP: Beginning Social Skills
SKILL 3: Ending a conversation

Steps	Trainer Notes
1. Think about whether it is time to end the conversation.	Time constraints, the other person looks like they want to finish (observe body signals).
2. Think about what you can say.	Summarize, explain why you need to end the conversation.
3. Wait for a break in the conversation.	Refer back to various steps in the skill of listening.
4. Make a friendly closing remark.	Discuss verbal and nonverbal closings (hand wave, shaking hands, comment that you enjoyed talking).

Suggested Content for Modeling Displays

A. Neighborhood: Leaving the park, where you have been talking with someone.

B. Home: You have been talking on the telephone with a relative and realize that you have to leave for an appointment.

C. Work: Your coffee break time is over, and you need to get back to your work station after chatting with a co-worker about a family problem.

Comments

Trainers and trainees alike can think of many people they know who just like to talk and talk. Perhaps you even have one or more of these individuals in your group. We have chosen to include this as a separate skill to emphasize the notion of the graceful ending to a conversation, which leaves open the prospect of another conversation in the future.

GROUP: Beginning Social Skills
SKILL 4: Asking for help

Steps	Trainer Notes
1. Decide what the problem is.	Help the trainee pinpoint and clarify the problem, getting rid of extraneous issues.
2. Decide if you want help for the problem.	Help the trainee decide whether the problem can be solved independently.
3. Decide who would be best to help you.	Here the trainee should review several possible helpers and select one.
4. Ask for help in a sincere way.	This step should include explaining the problem to the helper.

Suggested Content for Modeling Displays

A. Neighborhood: You need to get a bulky furniture item into your apartment.

B. Home: You need help with a personal problem.

C. Work: You are having difficulty understanding some of your job duties.

Comments

In working on this skill, trainers need to be alert to the variety of personality styles of trainees in your group. Many trainees are well practiced at dependent behaviors and will tend to ask for help with things that they are capable of doing for themselves. On the other hand, there are trainees who are withdrawn socially, who will tend to give up at a task that requires help.

GROUP: Beginning Social Skills
SKILL 5: Following instructions

Steps	Trainer Notes
1. Listen carefully to the instructions.	Trainers should refer trainees back to the steps learned in the skill of listening.
2. Ask about anything you don't understand.	Trainees should be encouraged to say things like "Do you mean _____ ?"
3. Repeat the instructions to yourself immediately.	Trainees should use their own words. Encourage writing down the instructions if they are complicated.
4. Do what you have been asked to do.	

Suggested Content for Modeling Displays

A. Neighborhood: You have been given instructions about how to get to the supermarket on the bus.

B. Home: You have been given instructions as to how to use a new kitchen appliance.

C. Work: You have a new supervisor who is explaining how things are to be done differently.

Comments

This skill involves complying with the request of another person. Group discussion might center around the issue of unreasonable requests. Here, you might even add a step that involves deciding whether the request is reasonable and whether the trainee wants to comply with the request.

GROUP: Beginning Social Skills
SKILL 6: Giving a compliment

Steps	Trainer Notes
1. Decide what you want to compliment about the other person.	Depending on the level of the group, trainers might want to focus on simple appearance or, with a more sophisticated group, on more psychologically-oriented traits.
2. Decide what you want to say.	Group discussion can focus on ways in which to compliment another person without both parties feeling embarrassed.
3. Choose a good time and place.	Focus here on whether there is a need for privacy or a special setting.
4. Give the compliment.	Trainers should focus on sincerity, friendliness.

Suggested Content for Modeling Displays

A. Neighborhood: You compliment a neighbor on how he or she looks.

B. Home: You compliment a relative on how he or she always makes you feel better.

C. Work: You compliment a supervisor on how he or she explains new tasks so clearly.

Comments

As with many other skills, content areas for both modeling and role playing can emerge from in-group situations. Trainees can compliment one another regarding progress made, new hairdos, clothes, accomplishment of behavioral tasks, and many other things.

GROUP: Beginning Social Skills
SKILL 7: Saying "thank you"

Steps	Trainer Notes
1. Decide if the other person has done something you feel thankful for.	This may be a compliment paid to the trainee, a favor, or a gift.
2. Think about ways to express your thanks.	Trainers can focus on verbal aspects of saying thanks, as well as on notions of doing something in return.
3. Choose the right time and place.	Issues of need for privacy, appropriate setting, other person's attention can be discussed.
4. Express your thanks.	Focus on sincerity, friendliness.

Suggested Content for Modeling Displays

A. Neighborhood: You respond to a store clerk's help in finding you the merchandise you are looking for.

B. Home: You respond to a relative's compliment about your new hairdo.

C. Clinic/hospital: You thank a nurse for helping you when you had a problem.

Comments

As with most skills, the sophistication level of your group will guide what you do with this skill. At its most basic level, trainees can work on saying "thank you" for a variety of things: compliments paid to them, help that has been given to them, or someone holding a door open. At a higher level, this skill can be used to help trainees work toward being more aware and supportive of many individuals in their environment.

GROUP: Beginning Social Skills
SKILL 8: Apologizing

Steps	Trainer Notes
1. Decide if you would like to apologize for something you did.	Brainstorm about things that warrant an apology (e.g., making an error, interrupting someone, breaking something that belongs to someone else).
2. Think of different ways you could apologize.	Discuss how to make the apology fit the offense.
3. Choose the best time and place and make your apology.	Discuss issues of private versus public apology, minimizing the delay between the offense and the apology.

Suggested Content for Modeling Displays

A. Home: It is late at night, and you are watching television. Your roommate comes in and tells you that the television was so loud it woke her up.

B. Work: You are an hour late for work. This is the second time this has happened in a week.

C. Clinic/hospital: Your friend has told you that he is very depressed. You know that he has tried to harm himself in the past, and so you tell his doctor what he has told you. In doing so, you have betrayed your friend's confidence.

Comments

Some trainees in your group probably apologize for everything, even things they have not done. Others do not seem to notice when they have committed even the most major offenses. In teaching this skill, group leaders should be aware of both extremes, because sometimes you will actually need to teach some trainees to apologize less (helping them to see in Step 1 that they have done nothing that warrants an apology).

GROUP: Skills for Dealing with Feelings
SKILL 9: Expressing your feelings

Steps	Trainer Notes
1. Tune in to what is going on in your body that helps you know what you are feeling.	Trainers can brainstorm with group members to develop a list of cues (blushing, tight muscles, etc.).
2. Think about what has happened to make you feel this way.	Scan recent events, thoughts.
3. Decide what you could call the feeling.	Here, again, a list can be generated by the group.
4. Think about different ways to express your feeling and pick one.	Consider possibilities such as talking about it, doing some physical activity, walking away from highly charged situation.

Suggested Content for Modeling Displays

A. Work: You have just had a disagreement with a co-worker and you begin making mistakes on your job.

B. Home: Your parents start discussing your emotional problems at a family gathering.

C. Clinic/hospital: Your therapist has told you something he says is important, and you can't follow it.

Comments

Isolating feelings, labeling feelings, and expressing them in satisfying and prosocial ways are probably some of the most challenging tasks undertaken by psychiatric patients. Although a skill-training approach might seem rather simplistic, there is much research to support that self-reflection enables the individual to slow down, label feelings more accurately, and respond less impulsively.

Group leaders might want to take this skill and focus an entire session on a single feeling, such as expressing affection, expressing anger, and the like. Modeling displays could be developed around these particular issues.

GROUP: Skills for Dealing with Feelings
SKILL 10: Understanding the feelings of others

Steps	Trainer Notes
1. Observe the other person's words and actions.	Notice tone of voice, posture, expressions, content.
2. Think about what the other person might be feeling.	Group leaders can brainstorm with their groups and develop a list of emotions and then help the trainee to find the emotion that fits with the other person's nonverbal and verbal cues.
3. Think about ways to show you understand what he or she is feeling.	Group leaders might ask trainees how they like to be treated when they are experiencing the feeling being described.
4. Decide on the best way and do it.	

Suggested Content for Modeling Displays

A. Neighborhood: Your next door neighbor's father has just died.

B. Home: Your spouse has just been laid off from work.

C. Work: There's a new person at work, and she's having a hard time catching on to some of her duties.

Comments

This skill is well known by the term *empathy*. Many group members will never be able to truly feel empathic in their interpersonal relationships but can be taught to behave more appropriately than they have in the past. In a more psychologically minded group, this skill can be the springboard for development of a better appreciation of significant others in their lives.

GROUP: Skills for Dealing with Feelings
SKILL 11: Preparing for a stressful conversation

Steps	Trainer Notes
1. Imagine how you will feel during the conversation.	Trainers will want to refer back to the steps learned in expressing feelings to help trainees isolate and label how they feel.
2. Think about how the other person will feel.	Trainers can refer back to understanding the feelings of others.
3. Think about different ways the conversation could go.	Trainees can rehearse different approaches, using various group suggestions.
4. Choose the best approach and try it.	

Suggested Content for Modeling Displays

A. Home: You may be laid off from your job. You need to tell your parents (spouse, roommate) about this.

B. Clinic/hospital: You have stopped taking your medication and need to tell your doctor about this. You have already missed several appointments because you don't want to have to face this.

C. Neighborhood: You don't have your rent money, and the rent is already overdue. You have been staying away from home to avoid meeting up with the landlord.

Comments

In teaching this skill, trainers can focus on the likelihood of trainee behavior influencing the outcome of the stressful conversation. Group feedback can be used in helping the trainee to select the approach that is most likely to produce a positive (or less negative) result.

GROUP: Skills for Dealing with Feelings
SKILL 12: Reacting to failure

Steps	Trainer Notes
1. Decide if you have failed.	Leaders can discuss issues of living up to one's own expectations and the expectations of others.
2. Think about the personal reasons and circumstances that contributed to your failure.	Group leaders can be helpful in assisting trainees in striking a balance between self-blame and blaming everyone but themselves.
3. Think about different ways of approaching the situation next time.	Some examples might include working harder, asking for help, or using a different method.
4. Decide whether you want to try again.	Group discussion can focus on whether another try is realistic or whether another failure experience is likely.

Suggested Content for Modeling Displays

A. Neighborhood: A store in your neighborhood has a "Help Wanted" sign. You have applied for the job but have gotten no response.

B. Clinic/hospital: You ask the nurse to decrease the frequency of your clinic appointments, as you feel you have been doing better. You are told that you are not doing much better and should continue with the same schedule.

C. Work: Your boss gave you some new job responsibilities a few weeks ago. You were happy about the chance to move on to more complicated work. This morning, he told you to go back to your previous job.

Comments

Failure is an all too common experience in the lives of psychiatric patients. Assessing a failure experience in a realistic way, without an exacerbation of psychiatric symptoms, might be one goal of teaching this skill. In a more sophisticated group, this goal might actually be the focus of group discussion.

GROUP: Assertiveness Skills
SKILL 13: Standing up for your rights

Steps	Trainer Notes
1. Tune in to whether you are dissatisfied and would like to stand up for yourself.	Trainers can review the skill of expressing your feelings, looking in particular at angry feelings. Awareness of physiological cues is often important here.
2. Think about what happened to make you feel dissatisfied.	Scan recent events, thoughts.
3. Think about ways in which you might stand up for yourself, and choose one.	Alternatives might include expressing your feelings, asking for help from an authority figure, or persuading others to join you in your point of view.
4. Take your stand in a direct and reasonable manner.	Trainers should help trainees focus on their manner of presentation and what message is conveyed through their style.

Suggested Content for Modeling Displays

A. Work: You have been disciplined unfairly by your supervisor.

B. Home: Your mother has gone into your room and looked at some private papers.

C. Clinic/hospital: You are in an elevator and hear some staff people talking about another patient.

Comments

Many volumes have been written about this skill, also known as *assertiveness*. As it is described in this skill, the activating element is the sense of dissatisfaction with events. We differentiate it from expression of angry feelings, because the action goes beyond simple expression of feelings.

GROUP: Assertiveness Skills
SKILL 14: Helping others

Steps	Trainer Notes
1. Decide if the other person might need or want your help.	Group leaders can refer back to the skill of understanding the feelings of others, asking group members to "put yourself in the other person's shoes."
2. Think of the ways you could be helpful.	Encourage trainees to brainstorm on this.
3. Offer to help in a friendly way.	Group members should be sensitive to the other person's wishes, especially the possibility that the offer might be refused.

Suggested Content for Modeling Displays

A. Home: Your spouse comes home from work particularly tired. You offer to do a chore that he or she typically does.

B. Work: Your co-worker has had a death in the family. You tell your supervisor that you would be glad to collect money for flowers.

C. Neighborhood: Your neighbor is carrying a heavy package. You offer to help carry it.

Comments

Psychiatric patients are notorious for being helpees and not helpers. We encourage group leaders to use this skill as a vehicle for enhancing trainees' self-esteem.

GROUP: Assertiveness Skills
SKILL 15: Giving instructions

Steps	Trainer Notes
1. Define what needs to be done.	Group discussion can focus on how to clarify and concretize a task.
2. Figure out who can do the task.	This step will depend on what kind of task is being discussed and in what kind of setting (e.g., does the task require particular skills? Is the main actor in a work situation?).
3. Tell the other person exactly how to do the task.	Encourage trainees to be as specific as possible, as they did in Step 1.
4. Ask the other person for his or her reactions.	Emphasize good listening skills.
5. Change or repeat your instructions if you need to.	This goes back to Step 4 and depends on whether the other person understands the task and agrees to do it.

Suggested Content for Modeling Displays

A. Work: You have been working at your job for 6 months. A new person has just been hired, and your supervisor asks you to explain one of the job duties.

B. Home: Your friend will be watching your pet while you are away for the weekend.

C. Neighborhood: You are heading up a committee and have to divide up the jobs.

Comments

In discussing this skill, some group members will be likely to feel that it is easier to do something themselves rather than asking someone else to do it. Giving instructions implies that the person knows more about the task than the other person, and as such, a certain amount of self-esteem is required. In a particularly passive group, group discussion can focus on skills of each group member and in what areas they could give instructions.

GROUP: Assertiveness Skills
SKILL 16: Making a complaint

Steps	Trainer Notes
1. Decide what the complaint is.	Making a complaint assumes that someone or something has caused a problem for the trainee. Here trainees can discuss what kinds of items warrant a complaint.
2. Decide whom to tell.	Choosing a person who can help to resolve a complaint can frequently present a problem. Some trainees will be likely to choose any trusted person, whether or not that person has anything to do with the problem.
3. Choose a good time and place.	Look at issues of attention, privacy.
4. Make your complaint.	Trainees can focus on making their complaint as well as suggesting a resolution to the problem at hand.

Suggested Content for Modeling Displays

A. Neighborhood: A person who lives in the building next door is throwing trash in front of your house.

B. Home: A family member is looking around in your room without permission.

C. Work: A co-worker is blaming you for errors that you have not committed.

Comments

In your group will probably be trainees at both ends of the spectrum on this skill. You will have some trainees who complain to everyone about everything that goes wrong in their lives. At the other end of the spectrum will be trainees who do not complain to anyone about any-thing, no matter how serious the offense. Trainees can be assisted in working toward an appropriate level of self-assertion.

GROUP: Assertiveness Skills
SKILL 17: Answering a complaint

Steps	Trainer Notes
1. Listen to the complaint.	Discuss listening skills.
2. Ask about anything you don't understand.	Discuss using this step as a way of communicating a nondefensive position.
3. Decide what to do about the complaint.	Choices might involve apologizing, accepting blame, correcting a mistaken impression, or compromising.
4. State your ideas about the complaint and what can be done.	Discuss ways of being forthright and friendly.

Suggested Content for Modeling Displays

A. Home: A family member complains that you aren't doing your chores.

B. Work: A supervisor complains that you have not cleaned up after yourself at the end of the day.

C. Clinic: Your therapist complains that you are late for your appointment for the second time in a row.

Comments

This skill runs the gamut from defending oneself to accepting responsibility for something one has done. Trainers should engage group members in deliberating the choices available to them in Step 3, encouraging brainstorming from all group members.

GROUP: Assertiveness Skills
SKILL 18: Negotiation

Steps	Trainer Notes
1. Decide if you and the other person disagree about something.	Trainers can be helpful in isolating the content of the disagreement from the feelings of both parties.
2. Explain your position and your understanding of the other person's position.	Frequently, people tend to persist in their own view. In negotiation, the person negotiating needs to demonstrate that he or she understands both sides.
3. Ask the other person what he or she thinks about the problem.	

Suggested Content for Modeling Displays

A. Home: You just got paid for some overtime at work. You had your heart set on buying something for yourself when your wife tells you she wants to pay another bill.

B. Work: You have just figured out a new way to handle a complicated problem. The method seems to work. Your boss comes over to you and tells you that he wants you to go back to the old way of doing it.

C. Neighborhood: You have a new neighbor who works the evening shift. When she comes home from work, she puts the television on full blast. This has been waking you up every night for the past week.

Comments

Negotiation is a skill that introduces the concept of compromise. The individual doing the negotiation must be willing to give up something in order to get something. The person must also be able to understand and process what the other person is saying and feeling about their side of the story. The subtleties of using this skill well will be more meaningful to sophisticated clients.

GROUP: Assertiveness Skills
SKILL 19: Self-control

Steps	Trainer Notes
1. Tune in to what is going on in your body that helps you know you are angry and about to lose control.	Trainers can develop a list of cues, such as feeling hot, clenching teeth.
2. Think about what has happened to make you feel this way.	Scan recent events, thoughts.
3. Think about your choices: a. Leave the situation b. Give yourself time to calm down c. Talk about how you feel.	Trainees can add items to this list of choices.
4. Consider the choices and pick one.	Group members can discuss what methods have and have not worked in the past.

Suggested Content for Modeling Displays

A. Home: Your spouse has come home drunk and tries to pick a fight.

B. Work: You ask for a day off, and your boss says no.

C. Clinic/hospital: You look very tired when you get to the clinic. Everyone starts asking you if you have been drinking.

Comments

The steps in this skill are designed to help group members delay and reflect on their choices before reacting to an anger-provoking situation. In discussing this skill, group leaders can discuss the value of reflecting on choices, rather than acting impulsively.

GROUP: Assertiveness Skills

SKILL 20: Persuasion

Steps	Trainer Notes
1. Decide if you want to persuade someone about something.	Group members can generate a list of areas where persuasion is important (doing something your way, going someplace, evaluating events).
2. Tell the other person your idea.	Trainers may want to discuss how to do this in a convincing way, including clarity of presentation, how the trainee feels about what he or she wants.
3. Ask the other person what he or she thinks about it.	This requires use of listening skill.
4. Respond to any issues the other person has raised.	Trainee needs to show understanding of other points of view here, without necessarily giving in.
5. Ask the other person to think about what you said before making up his or her mind.	An important part of this skill is giving the respondent time to think things over.

Suggested Content for Modeling Displays

A. Home: You haven't been driving since your hospitalization. You want to convince your spouse that you can concentrate well enough to drive.

B. Work: You want to convince your boss that you can handle a more responsible job.

C. Neighborhood: You want to go to a ballgame but don't like to go by yourself. You try to convince your neighbor to go with you.

Comments

This skill is a very difficult one for individuals who are deficient in social skills. They may tend to be overly apologetic, talking themselves and others out of things very readily. Manner of presentation, elimination of apologetic statements, and tone of voice are some of the areas where group leaders can direct the attention of group members during role play.

In the last step, the main actor is instructed to delay in getting a response. This is intended to give the respondent time to think things over, rather than giving an immediate response. Research in persuasive techniques indicates that this tends to be an important component in being persuasive.

GROUP: Assertiveness Skills

SKILL 21: Responding to persuasion

Steps	Trainer Notes
1. Listen to the other person's position.	Steps in listening should be reviewed here, with particular emphasis on thinking about what is being said.
2. Think about your position.	Group members should be encouraged to distinguish their ideas from the ideas of others.
3. Compare your ideas with the ideas of the other person.	Trainers might develop a list of pros and cons for each position.
4. Decide which idea you like better and tell the other person about it.	Trainers can help trainees look at the variety of conclusions they can draw (agree, disagree, modify, postpone deciding).

Suggested Content for Modeling Displays

A. Home: The telephone rings, and it is a high-pressure salesperson.

B. Work: A co-worker tries to convince you to come to a party after work. You know that there will be drugs at the party.

C. Neighborhood: Your next door neighbor asks to borrow $20 until he gets paid. He already owes you money he promised to repay 2 weeks ago.

Comments

Passive trainees are ready targets for persuasive salespeople, neighbors, and family members, among others. In thinking through the steps in this skill, they can become more able to separate their own ideas from the ideas of others, which is the first step in resisting being pressured. Trainers should remember to encourage trainees to look at long-term consequences of any decisions that they make.

GROUP: Assertiveness Skills
SKILL 22: Dealing with group pressure

Steps	Trainer Notes
1. Think about what the group wants you to do.	At its most basic level, this involves the skill of listening. At its more subtle level, group members can be encouraged to discuss hidden agendas, undercurrents, body language, etc.
2. Think about the consequences of going along.	Here trainees can develop a list of pros and cons.
3. Decide what you want to do.	Group discussion can focus on how difficult it is to resist pressure, especially when faced by a powerful group (family, authority figures).
4. Think about how to tell the group what you have decided.	This might involve explanation, walking away, or a variety of already practiced assertiveness skills.
5. Tell the group what you have decided.	Group leaders can focus on how the trainee delivers the message.

Suggested Content for Modeling Displays

A. Home: Your family is pressuring you to break up with your boyfriend.

B. Work: You have missed a lot of work lately because of various doctors' appointments as well as court appearances. Although no one has confronted you directly, you are hearing lots of comments about whether you ought to quit your job.

C. Neighborhood: You have remained sober for the last 6 months. Some friends stop you on the street and try to talk you into coming with them to a neighborhood bar.

Comments

This skill is the group version of responding to persuasion. We have included it as a separate skill as this sort of pressure is sometimes more overwhelming than pressure coming from an individual. As with the earlier skill, group leaders should help trainees focus on differentiating their ideas from the ideas of others.

GROUP: Problem-solving Skills
SKILL 23: Setting priorities

Steps	Trainer Notes
1. Make a list of the things you would like to accomplish.	Encourage group members to brainstorm and develop an inclusive list of problems currently pressuring them.
2. Arrange your list in order from most important to least important.	
3. Do what you can to hold off on less pressing problems.	This may involve a telephone call, writing a letter, or deciding to postpone.
4. Concentrate on your most pressing problem.	Here we move into the problem-solving skill of concentrating on a task.

Suggested Content for Modeling Displays

A. Home: You have a number of chores to do. Just as you get started on one of them, a friend calls to see if you want to go to the movies.

B. Work: A co-worker has gone on vacation. Your boss asks you to take over her job as well as your own.

C. Clinic/hospital: You have been discussing a number of problems in your therapy session. When you leave your counselor's office, you feel overwhelmed with all the things you said you wanted to work on.

Comments

The process of setting problem priorities is one that comes almost automatically to many individuals. However, when the pressure of too many problems and too little time becomes overwhelming, making lists and taking deliberate steps to delay less pressing matters are often helpful.

GROUP: Problem-solving Skills
SKILL 24: Making decisions

Steps	Trainer Notes
1. Think about the problem that requires a decision.	Group discussion can focus on elaboration of various aspects of the problem.
2. Think about the possible decisions you could make.	Encourage the group to generate a number of alternatives.
3. Think about the consequences of each choice.	The person may have to gather information, or ask questions, or review past experiences.
4. Make a decision that is in your best interest.	Here the group member needs to weigh the information gathered above.

Suggested Content for Modeling Displays

A. Home: Your doctor has recommended that you leave your job, which has become too stressful for you. If you do this, you will have to move back with your family. You know that this is also stressful for you.

B. Work: You have the opportunity to move to the night shift at work. Although it will mean more money, it also means that you will see your spouse much less. You are not sure if this will create more or less stress in your marriage.

C. Neighborhood: Your lease is up, and you are thinking about moving. There are pros and cons to staying put. Your place is a long walk from the bus, and there is no supermarket nearby. On the other hand, you have made friends with a few neighbors.

Comments

This skill focuses on reflectively weighing choices before making decisions. At the two extremes will be group members who forge ahead impulsively without weighing consequences, whereas others can do nothing but deliberate without deciding. Group leaders can foster a discussion between individuals at these two extremes.

GROUP: Problem-solving Skills
SKILL 25: Setting a goal

Steps	Trainer Notes
1. Decide what you would like to accomplish.	Group discussion can focus on whether the goal is realistic.
2. Collect information about how to reach your goal.	Group leaders might assign this as homework, encouraging group members to talk to relevant individuals, look things up. These conversations can be role played if indicated.
3. Think about the steps you will need to take to reach your goal.	Steps should be reviewed in order, with reference back to information collected in Step 2.
4. Decide if your goal is realistic and take your first step.	Although the realistic nature of the goal has already been discussed in Step 1, here we ask the trainee to go back through his or her planning process, assess it, revise it, and move ahead.

Suggested Content for Modeling Displays

A. Home: Your apartment building is very dirty and noisy. You are thinking about moving.

B. Work: You have been thinking about changing jobs. Everything you look at requires a high school diploma. You decide to look into obtaining one.

C. Clinic/hospital: You have been taking the same medicine for your psychiatric problem for the past 2 years. You wonder if you still need it, and you are thinking you would like to be off all medicine.

Comments

This skill has many aspects in common with concentrating on a task. In fact, the first step in the next skill asks the individual to set a goal. We have differentiated them in our modeling displays by including larger, and sometimes more vaguely defined, issues in this skill. Once goals are set, the individual tasks can be tackled using the next skill.

GROUP: Problem-solving Skills
SKILL 26: Concentrating on a task

Steps	Trainer Notes
1. Set a reasonable goal.	Group members can help individuals to be realistic in their expectations of what they can accomplish. Discussion can focus on what happens when goals are unrealistic.
2. Decide on a reasonable time schedule.	The word "reasonable" is used again in this step, as trainees need to focus on when to work and how long to work. Too often, individuals overestimate what is realistic.
3. Gather the materials you need.	When this aspect of a task is not planned, the person is faced with interruptions (e.g., trips to the store, telephone calls).
4. Select a place to work.	Plan to minimize distraction, interruptions.
5. Decide whether you are ready and begin the task.	This involves reviewing the previous steps to make sure all relevant planning has been done.

Suggested Content for Modeling Displays

A. Home: Your apartment is a mess. You are having company tomorrow and need to do some cleaning.

B. Work: Your boss has recommended that you bid for two jobs that are vacant. Both would mean more money. Each job requires you to fill out a form.

C. Neighborhood: You have a budget for buying furniture for your room. You have a mattress but nothing else.

Comments

Group leaders should focus on taking a big job, breaking it down into manageable steps, and concentrating on these steps. Issues of motivation and reinforcement for accomplishing difficult or onerous tasks can also be discussed. As with a number of other skills in this problem-solving section, there is no interpersonal component in practicing this skill. Role playing per se may be more difficult with problem-solving skills, with group leaders focusing more on writing lists, group discussion, making schedules, and the like. Homework assignments are a major aspect of working on this group of skills.

GROUP: Problem-solving Skills
SKILL 27: Rewarding yourself

Steps	Trainer Notes
1. Decide if you have done something that deserves a reward.	Group leaders can brainstorm with the group about what warrants self-reward.
2. Decide what you could say to reward yourself.	Discussion can focus on purpose of self-praise.
3. Decide what you can do to reward yourself.	Categories of rewards, such as buying something, or doing a desirable activity, can be discussed.
4. Reward yourself.	This should include something from Step 2 and Step 3.

Suggested Content for Modeling Displays

A. Home: You have done a really thorough job studying for a test.

B. Neighborhood: You have recently moved into a new neighborhood. You were very lonely in the place you lived last. Today you made a point of introducing yourself to two people who live next door.

C. Work: Your supervisor is new. The former supervisor was someone who always complimented your work. The new one only talks to you when something is wrong. You notice that you are feeling a bit down about this, even though you are doing a good job, and the criticisms are not frequent occurrences.

Comments

A number of standard principles apply to self-reward. These should be discussed with trainees, along with their rationale.
1. Reward yourself as soon as possible after a job well done.
2. Reward yourself after, not before, the task has been accomplished.
3. The better the job, the greater the reward.
This skill could really have been included as a skill for dealing with feelings. Group leaders should include it where it seems most applicable.

Chapter 5

Managing Problematic Behaviors

The major task for Structured Learning trainers is to conduct groups according to specific guidelines and procedures. The overall goal of these groups is to help participants learn important skills. Behaviors that interfere with this learning process are viewed as problematic. This chapter describes a number of problematic behaviors that may occur in Structured Learning groups and illustrates several useful techniques for managing these behaviors so as to minimize their potentially negative impact on the progress of the group.

Structured Learning groups more closely resemble classes in school than they do traditional psychotherapy groups. Group leaders are often referred to as "trainers" and group members are frequently called "trainees." Particularly in mental health settings, participants seem to prefer to call the activity a "class" rather than a "group" or "therapy," these latter terms being reserved for more traditional, less structured psychotherapies. This is not to suggest that the trainers should ignore what they have learned about group dynamics or about group psychotherapy. However, instead of focusing primarily on the dynamics of the group, trainers attend to the Structured Learning procedures as their first consideration, attempting to incorporate within that format awareness of participants' feelings, interpersonal conflicts, power struggles, and other factors that might surface in the group situation.

In discussing the management of problematic behaviors that might occur in the context of a Structured Learning group, the emphasis is placed on decreasing or eliminating those behaviors that tend to interfere with the ongoing group procedures (*behavioral excesses*) and/or increasing those behaviors that, when they occur, contribute to a group's progress (*behavioral deficits*). The term *resistance* is generally not used in describing problematic behaviors that might appear in a Structured Learning group. Resistance is usually dealt with in the context of psychodynamic psychotherapies as unconscious and conscious forces that obstruct the progress of psychotherapy. The term resistance suggests that "the problem" is caused by something (resistance) that resides within the personality of the patient. In Structured Learning, problematic behaviors are dealt with by the trainers through modification of the training environment so as to keep the group on its prescribed course.

Although the fit may not be exact, the following are some major examples of excessive behaviors:

1. Hyperactivity (e.g., pacing, self-verbalizations)
2. Aggressive or impulsive behaviors (e.g., threatening others, yelling)
3. Attention-seeking behaviors (e.g., drawing the group's attention away from task at hand and onto self)
4. Emotional lability (e.g., inappropriate laughing, crying)
5. General disruption (e.g., interrupting ongoing activity, using profanity inappropriately, teasing)

Frequent types of deficient behaviors that may occur in Structured Learning groups include:

1. Negativism (e.g., refusing to participate, missing groups, walking out of group)
2. Inattentiveness (e.g., daydreaming, hallucinating)
3. Apathy and withdrawal (e.g., unable or unwilling to enter into group discussion, not caring)
4. Anxiety (e.g., fearfulness, afraid to speak up)
5. Verbal inadequacies (e.g., limited intellectual functioning)

This does not purport to be an exhaustive list or categorization of all problematic behaviors that could occur in a Structured Learning group. Nor is there a precise match or formula to select particular behavior management techniques for use with specific behaviors. However, there is clinical and research support for using certain classes of techniques with broad categories of behaviors. These can be divided into three large groupings:

1. *Behavior modification techniques.* Based on the use of principles of reinforcement, these techniques have been used both to decrease excessive behaviors and to increase infrequent behaviors.
2. *Instructional techniques.* These have been used to teach appropriate in-group behaviors that appear to be absent from the trainee's behavioral repertoire.

3. *Relationship-based techniques.* Often used to reduce threats or other interferences to adequate performance, these techniques are frequently used in conjunction with other behavior modification or instructional techniques.

In order to illustrate the specific techniques that may be used to manage problematic behaviors that might occur in a Structured Learning group, the remainder of this chapter is devoted to concrete examples that demonstrate these three broad categories of behavior management tools.

BEHAVIOR MODIFICATION TECHNIQUES

Increasing Desirable Behaviors

Reinforcement. Behaviors that are rewarded or reinforced tend to increase and be maintained. Trainees who fail to perform appropriate behaviors in or outside of the group may never have learned such behaviors, or they may have been learned once but the behaviors have faded from use because of lack of reinforcement. Indeed, the nonverbal, formerly institutionalized chronic psychiatric patient may have once learned how to make requests or assert him- or herself. Because these kinds of behaviors were generally not rewarded in his or her former home on the ward of the psychiatric hospital, they eventually disappeared from his or her behavioral repertoire. The trainer's task for this trainee is to make such infrequent verbalizations rewarding so that they increase in the group and are attempted outside of the group.

Social Reinforcement. This is perhaps the most frequently used and most powerful technique that is available, both in and outside of the Structured Learning group. Using praise, attention, a smile, or a friendly "good job" greatly enhances the likelihood that the behavior being rewarded will be repeated. Hence, social reinforcement must be used carefully and strategically to reinforce only those behaviors that one wishes to occur more often.

> Although the group was making good progress through the skills, the trainers were disappointed in the meager amount of discussion between participants. It seemed as though the behaviors being practiced were not transferring to in-group socialization. And if the behaviors were not transferring to in-group discussion, it was most likely that generalization outside of group was minimal. On one particular day, the skill of making a complaint was being practiced. Several group members began a lively discussion about how they were always expected to go along with what their doctors and therapists wanted. Seizing this as an opportunity, the trainers praised the group members for the spontaneity of their discussion, suggesting that this kind of discussion greatly enhanced the learning in the group.

Material Reinforcement. Sometimes, trainees will require reinforcement even more tangible than social reinforcement. This was found with the early applications of learning principles to the modification of maladaptive behaviors in severely institutionalized and retarded persons. By providing such individuals with tangible rewards, researchers and clinicians found that these chronic patients would engage in desirable behaviors in order to receive food, candy, cigarettes, or privileges. Because not all of these patients responded to the same tangible rewards (i.e., not everyone liked candy or cigarettes), a system was developed that operated much the same way that money operates in the mainstream of society; that is, patients would earn tokens, chips, credits, or points for performing the infrequent but desirable behavior and could then exchange this "currency" for what the patient considered reinforcing, whether it was candy, cigarettes, or an off-grounds pass. Because tokens were often used as the rewards, this approach to material reinforcement came to be known as a *token economy.*

> In developing plans for their inpatient group, the two leaders reviewed the hospital records on the patients they planned to include. One of the issues was the passivity and poor motivation of most of the members. They decided to incorporate a token system in order to increase motivational level. Points would be earned for a variety of in-group tasks. A group trip would be planned once individuals had earned a set number of points.

Shaping. At first, the desirable behavior to be reinforced is rarely evidenced in a final form that might then be rewarded, either materially or socially. Indeed, one would be naive to assume that most skill-deficient trainees are able to produce appropriate behaviors once they are given the opportunity and encouragement to do so. Whereas this may be the case for some whose primary difficulties are best described as behavioral inhibitions rather than behavioral deficits, it is probably not true for most of the participants in Structured Learning groups. Therefore, it makes little sense to wait for the polished, appropriate behavior to emerge, because that is unlikely to happen. The alternative strategy is to reward behaviors that begin to approach or approximate the target behaviors. By reinforcing these successive approximations, the final behavioral objective can be attained in a slow, gradual, incremental way. It would be futile to expect the regressed, withdrawn, nonverbal institutionalized patient to produce facile conversation right away. However, it might be possible to encourage the patient to establish eye contact, even briefly, and then to greet that attempt with lavish praise and/or material rewards.

Rose was mumbling and fidgeting during much of the first group meeting. During the second meeting, when asked to role play, she did not raise her voice above a whisper and was unable to sit still. The trainers decided to tackle one problem at a time and chose her nonverbal behavior, as it was a constant distraction throughout group meetings. They asked Rose to repeat Step 1, trying to sit as still as she could. They then had her repeat each remaining step, reminding her to sit still as she spoke. When she completed each step, they praised her for the improvement.

Self-reinforcement. This concept is described in three places in this book, including the discussion of transfer of training and maintenance in chapter 2, as a separate problem-solving skill in chapter 4, and here as a method of dealing with problematic behavior. This repetition highlights our conviction that self-reinforcement is an essential component of any behaviorally oriented program.

Both material reinforcement and social reinforcement are intended to be utilized within the context of the group experience to encourage trainees to perform behaviors that are otherwise absent or infrequent in their behavioral repertoires. Once these behaviors are evidenced, practiced, and rewarded within the group, trainees are encouraged to implement them outside of the group, assuming that their appropriate use in trainees' real-life environments will be greeted by naturally occurring reinforcements and positive outcomes. Unfortunately, this is not always the case. Behaviors that go unrewarded, particularly newly learned behaviors, typically become extinguished. To guard against this potential lack of real-life reinforcement, trainees can be taught explicitly to evaluate and to reward their own behaviors if and when they are performed successfully. They are taught to dispense both tangible self-rewards and positive self-statements as they demonstrate behaviors in real-life environments that they practiced in their Structured Learning groups. As they gradually assume more and more responsibility for evaluating and rewarding their own behaviors, trainees' dependence on evaluation and rewards from others can be diminished.

Andy was working on the skill of negotiation. He role played a negotiation situation with his wife regarding how to spend some of the Christmas money they had saved. When it came time to do it at home, his wife stood firm regarding how to spend the money. Andy came back to group rather disappointed as he told his story. The trainer asked Andy how he had done in following the steps. Andy agreed that he had done a good job and that he had tried to do something he would not even have attempted in the past. The trainer discussed with Andy how his ability to see that he had done a good job, and give himself a pat on the back for doing something difficult, was very important, even if the end result was not exactly what he wanted.

Decreasing Undesirable Behaviors

Extinction. Behaviors that are followed by reinforcement tend to be perpetuated. Likewise, behaviors that are not followed by reinforcement generally decrease or diminish in the frequency or intensity of their occurrence. This basic principle underlies most of the specific techniques for decreasing or minimizing the expression of undesirable, inappropriate behaviors in the Structured Learning group. By not rewarding behaviors that are disruptive, distracting, or otherwise inappropriate, trainers can focus on the appropriate behaviors that are being demonstrated. The primary way of doing this is through extinction coupled with redirection of group attention to on-task activities.

> MaryLou often took out her mirror and began combing her hair and putting on her makeup during group meetings. At first this got a good deal of group attention. When instructed to put her makeup away, MaryLou behaved as though she did not hear the group leader. Rather than let the situation escalate, the leader instructed group members to ignore Mary-Lou's behavior, telling them that by paying attention to it, they were encouraging it. Eventually, the behavior extinguished.

Trainers should not expect that disruptive behaviors that are no longer being attended to and reinforced will automatically and immediately be extinguished. Quite the contrary, the cliché that "things will get worse before they get better" is almost always true with regard to these initial attempts at extinction. After all, if the disruptive behaviors that were formerly attended to and rewarded are no longer successful in gaining those rewards, the trainee is likely to try harder to obtain the attention by escalating the inappropriate behaviors. It is only by consistently ignoring such behaviors that they will be extinguished.

> Harry would frequently laugh loudly when other group members were role playing. Group leaders had spoken to Harry about this to no avail and eventually resigned themselves to letting the behavior extinguish. When the group stopped attending to Harry's laughing, he began to laugh louder and longer. It was hard work focusing on the group task for several weeks. Eventually, the disruptive behavior dropped out.

Time out, or (temporary) exclusion, from the group is an even more powerful extinction technique that ensures that a trainee's inappropriate or disruptive behavior will not be reinforced. The trainee who continues to display disruptive behavior may be asked to sit in a different part of the room or even to leave the room until he or she is ready and able to behave appropriately. These exclusionary techniques should only be used after trainees have been forewarned about their possible use. This forewarning can be covered routinely as an aspect of the initial structuring of the group.

> After attempting to deal with Arnold's pacing through simple extinction for several weeks, the group leaders decided that they would try using time out. They spoke to Arnold at the end of a group meeting, telling him that if he needed to pace, he would have to go out into the hall. During the next group meeting, when Arnold got up to pace, the leaders reminded him of their plan. Arnold went out into the hall. He returned and sat down a few minutes later. The trainers noticed that right away there was a lessening of time spent pacing.

INSTRUCTIONAL TECHNIQUES

Basic to the Structured Learning approach is the assumption that desirable, prosocial behaviors may never have been learned, or if learned, these behaviors may not have been practiced sufficiently to be immediately available in trainees' behavioral repertoires. Trainees are assumed to be skill deficient, so that the appropriate social skills must be taught. This is also the assumption underlying a broad category of behavior management techniques. That is, it is assumed that some of the behavioral problems that occur within the context of the Structured Learning group simply reflect the fact that the appropriate in-group behaviors have not been learned adequately. Thus, trainees may be reverting to behaviors that are not appropriate to the Structured Learning group, even though they may be appropriate in other settings. Or, trainee inactivity or lack of participation in the group may indicate that they do not know what is expected of them. In these instances, the trainer's task is to provide the instructions that trainees need in order to function appropriately within the group setting.

Modeling and Role Playing

Just as social skills may be deficient, trainees may be deficient in the skills involved in following group procedures. Because the techniques utilized in Structured Learning involve modeling and role playing, it is logical that these same techniques should be useful in teaching appropriate in-group behaviors.

> Group members were having a difficult time giving feedback to one another after role playing. Rather than persist in trying to get more feedback, the group leaders decided to use modeling. After the next role play, they told the group that they would give the feedback and that group members should listen carefully as they did it. With succeeding role plays, the leaders asked group members to give feedback in the same manner as the leaders had done.

Providing Structure

The expectations as to what will go on in a Structured Learning group must be made as explicit as possible. It is often the case that some of the inappropriate behaviors that are observed in a group are attributable to trainees not understanding clearly what is expected of them. It is for this reason that the rules and procedures, expectations about participation—time schedules, absences, rewards, smoking, breaks—in short, all of the procedural aspects of the group, are covered completely at the outset and repeated as necessary. Trainees should have the security of knowing exactly what to expect in a Structured Learning group and exactly what will be expected of them.

> The trainers knew that group rules would be a problem with these particular trainees. They decided to write up the rules and put them on a poster that they could bring to group meetings. This way, the rules would be there each week for everyone to see.

Coaching and Prompting

In enacting various newly learned behaviors within a Structured Learning group, trainees may not be able to come up with the appropriate response to a particular situation presented to them. This is likely to occur in the context of a role play in which the person may not be able to think of the right thing to say in response to another trainee's statement. The trainers might choose to solicit suggestions from the rest of the group, or they might serve as coaches themselves, offering general ideas or even specific words or phrases. It is sometimes the case that the trainee who is new to role playing and/or anxious about his or her performance would benefit from occasional prompts or suggestions from the trainers. These tentative first attempts can be repeated until the trainee is more comfortable with the procedures and the specific verbal response.

> Bob seemed to become tongue-tied when he had to role play. The trainer decided to stand next to him and "feed" him his lines, so that he could begin to approximate what was expected of him. When he had repeated the lines he had been fed, the leader asked him to try it on his own. Bob performed awkwardly, but much better than before he was coached.

Simplification

Considerable effort has been devoted to making the Structured Learning procedures as concrete as possible so that even trainees who are quite limited intellectually or attentionally are able to participate appropriately. However, it is sometimes the case that the procedures have to be simplified even further. For example, if the trainee's deficits are so significant that he or she cannot manage a complete role play, then the sequence can be pared down even more. Simplification might involve limiting the number of behavioral steps, or using simpler language, or rote repetition of simple greetings.

Jane had very limited verbal skills. Her reading level was also quite low. The trainers found that a good way to help her role play was to list the steps with pictures next to them. She was very pleased to be able to participate more fully.

RELATIONSHIP-BASED TECHNIQUES

Virtually all schools and approaches to psychological treatment identify the relationship between the therapist and the patient (counselor and client) as a critically important element in effecting therapeutic change. For many theorists and therapists, this relationship is the most important ingredient in that change. For example, Carl Rogers, who influenced a whole generation of professional helpers and almost singlehandedly brought about a revolution in psychotherapeutic practice, based his theory of therapeutic personality change on the relationship between client and counselor (cf. Rogers, 1951). Even the behaviorists, who in the early days of behavior modification tended to disregard or greatly minimize the importance of the therapeutic relationship in favor of "the systematic application of learning theory," have generally come to acknowledge the central role that the helping relationship plays in facilitating positive outcomes (Goldstein, 1971). In light of this trend toward recognizing the importance of a positive relationship between trainers and trainees in bringing about therapeutic change, a number of specific techniques have been identified that have proved to be effective in enhancing the relationship aspects of the Structured Learning procedures.

Empathic Encouragement. Trainees who are not following the prescribed procedures or otherwise appear to be having difficulty participating appropriately in the Structured Learning group are likely to begin to behave more appropriately if they can be made to feel as if the trainer understands what they are going through and what they may be feeling. The trainer can communicate a sense of empathic encouragement by following a series of steps, as follows:

1. The trainer offers the trainee the opportunity to explain in detail his
    or her difficulty in participating as instructed and listens
    nondefensively.
2. The trainer expresses an understanding of the trainee's behavior.
3. If appropriate, the trainer responds that the trainee's view is a viable
    alternative.
4. The trainer restates his her or view, with supporting reasons and
    probable outcomes.
5. The trainer expresses the appropriateness of delaying a resolution of
    the problem.
6. The trainer urges the trainee to try to participate as best as he or she
    can.

> Blanche was refusing to role play the skill of persuading others. When ev-
> eryone had had a turn, the group leader again turned to Blanche and asked
> her to role play. Blanche said she did not want to role play because she
> would never use the skill. She stated that she had always been a shy person
> and that she just went along with her husband's way of doing things. The
> trainer stated that she understood Blanche's perspective and that fre-
> quently it was a good idea to go along and not make waves, but that the
> skill could be useful in some circumstances. The leader then turned to the
> group and asked if group members would help come up with some cir-
> cumstances in which Blanche would need to persuade someone of some-
> thing. Arthur stated that if Blanche was thinking about getting a job, she
> would have to convince the boss to hire her. The trainer suggested to
> Blanche that this was certainly a good place to consider using the skill and
> suggested Blanche think about role playing a job interview at the next
> group meeting. Blanche agreed to think about it.

Problem Identification. Trainees often have difficulty categorizing, labeling, or otherwise identifying the problems they are experiencing in a way
that is meaningful to them. Without such an ability or a system for identifying problems, trainees may opt not to participate because they cannot
see that their discomfort or difficulties relate to the procedures being enacted in the Structured Learning group. Structured Learning is particularly conducive to assisting with problem identification by using the
Structured Learning skills to help trainees both identify and label their
difficulties. Once this has been done, the steps for dealing with the difficulties are immediately available.

> Charles had been fidgeting and pacing through the first 20 minutes of the
> group. The trainers had been trying to deal with it through extinction.
> When Charles began swearing, it became clear that Charles' problematic
> behavior was not about to drop out. When one of the trainers asked
> Charles what was bothering him, Charles was unable to explain. The
> trainer suggested to Charles that he was having difficulty giving a name to
> what he was feeling. At the same time, the trainer began putting the steps
> for "identifying and labeling your emotions" on the board. As the group

began to talk about the skill, Charles started to pay attention. It was no surprise to anyone that Charles was angry.

Threat Reduction. For many trainees, participation in a group experience may prove to be anxiety provoking. This anxiety may become manifest in a variety of ways: withdrawal, hyperactivity, verboseness, defiance, or disruptiveness. Trainers must anticipate this anxiety and threat and be prepared to reduce it as soon as possible. Any and all of the specific techniques in this chapter may prove helpful in this regard. Certainly, the environment in the group should be made as safe, structured, and predictable as possible. At times, trainers need to provide structure, guidance, coaching, reassurance, and even physical contact. Peer acceptance and support is often particularly important for anxious, fearful trainees.

> The ward had been chaotic all week following an incident in which an angry patient assaulted a staff member. Although there had been a number of ward meetings after the incident, the group leaders could feel that there was still a good deal of anxiety in the group. Rather than get right into the material they had planned to cover, they decided to address the anxiety. The small size of the group enabled a number of the less verbal patients to express their feelings about the incident, and eventually the group was able to go on to work on their new skill.

Peer Support. Any group in which the majority of its members do not support the goals or procedures of the group is almost always doomed to failure. Conversely, the support and encouragement of one's peers is of critical importance in the success of any endeavor, including appropriate participation in a Structured Learning group. Whereas it is true that the trainer's status carries with it a certain power, as well as the responsibility to structure and direct the group, trainers should be especially attuned to the power of the peer group in managing behaviors within the group. This potential for peer support must be nurtured carefully and strategically so that it can be used to encourage appropriate behaviors and to discourage inappropriate behaviors. This peer support may be viewed as a specific type of threat reduction, helping the anxious trainee to begin to see the group as a safe, supportive place. Likewise, the group members can be the most potent enforcers of group rules and group procedures, thus encouraging or influencing trainees to behave appropriately.

> Carlton was missing a number of group meetings and showing up late for the rest. The group leader had spoken to him privately about the problem, but this seemed to have no impact. The trainer decided that it was time to bring it up in the group. When Carlton came in, and noisily took his seat, the leader asked the group members for their reactions. No one said anything. Eventually, Grace spoke up and told Carlton that she missed him

when he wasn't there. She said she knew he had problems with transportation and with taking care of his mother. Several other group members chimed in that when Carlton wasn't there, they missed his sense of humor. Carlton seemed to brighten up. On further discussion, he said that he did not think anybody noticed when he was missing. After that session, his attendance began to improve. The trainer made a point of commenting on his improvement and encouraged the group to continue to support the change.

SUMMARY

Problematic behaviors that may occur within a Structured Learning group are those behaviors that detract from the progress of the group in accomplishing its goals. They are not seen as inherent within the trainees, but rather as byproducts of the group situation. Broadly, these problematic behaviors have been characterized as behavioral excesses and behavioral deficits. Although there is no absolute formula for applying specific behavior management techniques to remedy particular problematic behaviors, three major categories of management techniques have been discussed: behavior modification techniques, instructional techniques, and relationship-based techniques. Examples have been presented that help trainers to identify problematic behaviors and to respond to them as quickly and effectively as possible.

Chapter 6

Structured Learning In Use

AN INITIAL STRUCTURED
LEARNING SESSION

The following transcript depicts a Structured Learning group meeting for the first time at a community mental health center. This particular group consists of eight trainees and two trainers. At a weekly staff meeting, Jack Bianco, the social worker, and Debbie Johnson, the nurse at the center, announced that they were going to offer a 12-session "Basic Social Skills" group, and staff were asked to identify and nominate prospective group members. Notices of the group were also posted so that patients attending the center could apply directly for possible inclusion in the group. Debbie and Frank interviewed all potential group members individually in order to describe the group and to assess their interest and appropriateness. They were looking for people who had difficulty in initiating and maintaining even casual social relationships. Applicants were asked to complete skill checklists, as were the center's staff members who knew the applicants. Through this process, the final selection of group members was made.

The goals of the first session were to create a comfortable atmosphere in the group, to describe Structured Learning procedures, to begin to demonstrate the relevance of improved social skills to trainees' lives, and to establish group norms. Recognizing that most of this is best done by demonstration rather than by description, the trainers minimized the didactic aspects of their introduction.

Trainer 1: Good morning. For those of you who don't know me, I'm Jack Bianco, and I'm a social worker here at the center. I'm going to be one of the trainers for this "social skills group." The other trainer is Debbie Johnson.

Trainer 2:   Hi. I'm Debbie Johnson, and I'm a nurse at the center. Since we're going to be working together for the next 12 weeks, I thought that we might begin by introducing ourselves and telling a little about ourselves. I don't think all of you know each other. As I said, I'm Debbie Johnson, and I'm a nurse. And, let's see, one of the things I like to do when I'm not working is to go hiking and backpacking. Blanche, why don't you introduce yourself and maybe tell the group one thing that you like to do.

Blanche: Yes, ma'am. They told me to come here. After I left the hospital.

Trainer 2:   And are there things that you like to do in your spare time?

Blanche: I don't mind cleaning.

Trainer 2:   Thank you, Blanche. And welcome to the group. Arthur?

Arthur: Arthur. My name's Arthur. I live at home.

Trainer 1:   And is there something that you like to do in your spare time, like a hobby?

Arthur: TV.

Trainer 1:   Thank you, Arthur, and welcome to the group. Mary, will you introduce yourself?

Mary: Do I have to?

Trainer 1:   You certainly don't have to, but I'm sure that the people in the group would like to meet you and begin to get to know you.

Mary: I'm Mary, and I live at Maple Lodge, and my roommate's name is Jenny and I wish she was here with me.

Trainer 1:   Thanks, Mary. We're glad you could come today. Frank?

Frank: My name's Frank, and I'm here because my therapist suggested that I come. I don't like to go to too many places since my wife died.

Trainer 2:   Well, we're glad you decided to get out today and come to the group. Keisha?

Keisha: I'm Keisha, and I don't get out much either. But that's because I got babies at home. I don't have time for much else.

Trainer 2:   Thanks for coming, Keisha. Lamar, would you introduce yourself and maybe tell us something you like to do?

Lamar: My name's Lamar, and I work in the file room at Federated. I live by myself, and I like to ride my bike when the weather's good.

Trainer 1:   Thanks, Lamar. And thanks for mentioning your bike riding. Flo, would you introduce yourself to the group?

Flo: I'm very nervous about being here. I'd much rather be at home, watching TV. When we discussed this before, you told me I didn't have to stay if I got too nervous.

Trainer 1:   That's certainly true, Flo. You don't have to stay if you don't want to. But we're very pleased that you were able to come and we hope that you will stay. Curt, would you introduce yourself, please?

Curt: I'm Curt, and I'm here because my probation officer said it would be good for me. Hey, I'm willing to go along with the program.

Trainer 1:   Thanks, Curt, and the rest of you. This looks like a good group. I'm sure we'll all get to know each other as the group goes on. Since you all told a little about yourselves, let me say a couple of things about myself. I've been here at the center for about 4 years. Outside of work, let's see. I like to fish and do home repairs. And, as some of you know, I like to be called by my first name, Jack. How about you, Debbie?

Trainer 2:   Yes, please call me Debbie. And let me tell you a couple of things about the group. We'll be meeting in this room at this time for 12 weeks, counting today. As you'll see, there are a lot of important things that we want to accomplish, so that it's very important that you come to all of the meetings and that you come on time. The group will last 1 hour each meeting, so we'll need to get started right away if we're going to cover everything we have planned for each session. If you're very sick, or if there's an emergency, please contact Jack or me. Otherwise, we'll expect you here. Oh, one other thing. You probably know that the center became "Smoke Free" a couple of months ago. As an ex-smoker I know that can be tough if you still smoke, but try to hang in there.

Trainer 1:   When we talked to each of you before the group started, a couple of you wanted to know what we were planning to do in the group and how it might help you feel better. You know that the group is called a "Social Skills" group. What we mean by social skills are the kinds of things that help you to communicate more comfortably with other people—how to talk to people and how to be a good listener; how to tell other people what you need and how to let them know what you're feeling. When people can do these things well, they usually feel better about themselves.

Trainer 2:   The way we're going to learn these skills is the same way we learn most things. Lamar, you said that you like to ride your bicycle when you're not working. If I didn't know how to ride a bike, do you think you could teach me?

Lamar: I don't know. I guess I could.

Trainer 2:   OK. What would you do first?

Lamar: If you never rode a bike before? Mine's a 12-speed, so I'd have to show you how the gears work. And how to get on, and use the brakes.

Trainer 2:   So the first thing you would do is *show* me how to do it (writes the word "Show" on the chalkboard). And you also did something else: you broke it down into a number of *steps*—what you would do first, second, and so on (writes "Steps" on the board). What would you do next?

Lamar: Well, after I showed you how to get on, use the gears and brakes, and balance yourself, then you'd have to try it yourself. I might have to help you balance at first.

Trainer 2:   Good point! You'd ask me to *try* it (writes "Try" on the board), but you'd be there to help me if I needed it.

Lamar: Yeah, you might lose your balance the first time. But after that, you'd be OK.

Trainer 2:   And I'm sure I would appreciate your support. OK. Let's say that I tried it. What would you do next?

Lamar: Well, I'd be there, watching, and if you didn't use the gears right or something, I'd let you know.

Trainer 2:   So you'd *tell* me what I did right and what I did wrong (writes "Tell" on the board). Good. What else do I need to do to really learn how to ride a bike well?

Lamar: You need to keep practicing. Do it on your own.

Trainer 2:   Exactly! I'll need to *practice* (writes "Practice" on the board). Lamar, the way you were going to teach me to ride a bike is exactly the way we're going to learn social skills in here—show, try, tell and practice. Jack and I will show you good ways of using social skills, then help each of you try them. We'll tell you how you're doing and let you practice your new skills till they're really sharp.

Trainer 1:   Probably the best way to show you what we mean is to actually get started with an important social skill. We thought we'd begin with the skill of listening. A lot of times, when people are a little uncomfortable around other people, they have difficulty listening.

Flo: That's me.

Trainer 2:   It's true of lots of people. And what has been found is that people can learn to be better listeners. What we're going to do now is to show you how to improve your listening skills. In a couple of minutes, Jack and I are going to show you some examples of good listening. We're going to do this by going through the four steps that make up the skill of listening. The first thing you do when you want to listen is to "look at the person who is talking" (writes on the board). Next, you "think about what's being said" (writes on the board). The next thing that you do is "wait your turn to talk" (writes on board). Finally, you "say what you want to say" (writes on board). When you've done these steps, then you've performed the skill of listening.

Trainer 1:   Before we begin, let me pass out some skill cards. You'll see that the same steps that Debbie just wrote on the board are printed on the cards. We'd like you to follow along on the cards, or on the board, as we go through the skill to see if we've covered all the steps. OK. In this first example of the skill of listening, I'm going to pretend to be a person who's talking to his doctor about a new medication. Debbie will play the role of the doctor. Now, it's very important that I listen to the information and instructions that the doctor gives me. If there's anything that I'm not clear about, I need to be sure to ask and to let the doctor know about my concerns. So, it's real important that I listen to what the doctor says. Let's pretend that the doctor is sitting behind her desk—this table can be the desk—and I'm sitting in front of the desk. She's going to be talking to me about the prescription. Step 1 says, "Look at the person who is talking." I'll look right at Debbie, the doctor. OK , let's pick it up here.

Trainer 2 (as doctor):   I want you to take one of these pills with breakfast, one with lunch, and one with dinner, and take the last one right before bed.

Trainer 1:   The second step says to think about what is being said. Ordinarily, you would think this silently to yourself. But just so we all can know what's going on, I'll say it out loud. She's telling me to take the meds at mealtimes and before bed. I wonder what happens if I eat late, like when I work second shift. The third step says to wait your turn to talk.

Trainer 2 (as doctor):   You may find that once you start taking the medication, your mouth may become dry. If that lasts more than a couple of days, let me know. Also, some people get headaches while on these pills. Let me know that, too, if it happens. Any questions so far?

Trainer 1:   The fourth step says to say what you want to say. Yes doctor, there is one thing. Sometimes when I work second shift, I eat lunch much later, around four o'clock. Will that make a difference?

Trainer 2 (as doctor):   That's a very good question. I'm glad you were paying close attention. If you do have to eat your lunch later, I still want you to take the medication with your meals, particularly if you're going to be up later at night.

Trainer 1:   OK. Let's stop there. Did everyone see how we went through all of the steps for listening? Did we miss any?

Keisha: I think you got them all.

Trainer 2:   I'm glad you were watching closely, Keisha. Any comments or suggestions about what you saw?

Keisha: You both did real good. The doctor was very nice.

Trainer 2:   Thanks for the compliment and for your comments. Any other comments or suggestions? OK, let's try another example. This time Jack will pretend that he's my husband, coming home after a hard day at work. He's been having some problems on the job and really wants to talk to me about them, so I really need to listen. This time, how about if some of you look for particular steps. Curt, will you take Step 1? Mary, Step 2; Blanche, Step 3; and Arthur, Step 4. The rest of you watch carefully to see how well I perform the skill of listening.

(Trainers present a second modeling display.)

Trainer 1:   OK, that's it. Did Debbie go through all the steps? Curt, did she do Step 1?

Curt: Sure, she was looking right at you.

Trainer 1:   Yes, she was. Thanks, Curt. Step 2. Mary?

Mary: Mary, that's me.

Trainer 2:   Yes, Mary. Did I do Step 2? "Think about what is being said."

Mary: You were talking.

Trainer 2:   It's what we call, "thinking out loud," so that everyone can know what I'm thinking. You're right, usually I wouldn't talk out loud. Thanks for paying attention. Step 3. Blanche?

Blanche: Yes ma'am?

Trainer 2:   Step 3 says, "Wait your turn to talk." Did I wait?

Blanche: Yes, ma'am.

Trainer 2:   Thanks, Blanche. Yes, I tried to wait while my husband was speaking. And Step 4?

Arthur: That's me.

Trainer 2:   Right. Did I do Step 4?

Arthur: I don't know.

Trainer 1:   Anybody?

Frank: Yeah, Debbie asked you something about your boss.

Trainer 2:   That's exactly right! Thanks, Frank. Any other comments or suggestions? Do you think I was listening well?

Keisha: You did good. I wish it worked like that for me.

Trainer 2:   What do you mean?

Keisha: Like listenin' to your husband. I try to listen to mine, and he gets mad at me. I'm home most of the time with my babies, and that's hard enough without his yelling. I really do try.

Trainer 1:   Would you like to tell the group a little more about it? Maybe we can help you figure out and practice some other ways to handle these situations. Could you give us an example?

Keisha: I could give you 10 examples. Like last night, he comes home and right away he starts complaining and yelling. I know he's having a tough time trying to find work, but he doesn't have to take it out on me and the babies.

Trainer 1:   He just started complaining and yelling? What was going on?

Keisha: Well, Kenny was laid off about a month ago, and he's been looking for work and not finding any. So now he's getting worried and uptight. He's no fun to be with, let me tell you!

Trainer 1:   Maybe we can help you figure out how to handle that kind of situation better next time it comes up. Would you like to try?

Keisha: Sure. I need all the help I can get.

Trainer 2:   Good. Maybe if Kenny knows you're really listening to him he won't get so upset. Who in the group reminds you of Kenny?

Keisha: I guess Curt does. He's sort of smooth, like Kenny is most of the time. But when Kenny gets uptight he can be kinda nasty.

Trainer 2:   Curt, do you think you can play the part of Kenny? We'll give you some more information.

Curt: Hey, no problem.

Trainer 1:   OK. Keisha, when are you likely to be in a situation when it would be helpful to let Kenny know that you're listening to him?

Keisha: Every afternoon. Tomorrow. Next day. Until he finds a job.

Trainer 1:   So it could be tomorrow or the next day. Where does this take place?

Keisha: Front room of the apartment. He comes through the door, looks around, usually finds something wrong, and then starts on me and the kids. To tell you the truth, it's got so that I try not to be around. Or I stay in the kitchen with the kids and cook and watch TV.

Trainer 1:   What's Kenny likely to say when he comes in the door?

Keisha: Well, if I'm hiding in the kitchen he'll say, "Where the hell is everybody?" and then off he'll go.

Trainer 1:   Well, instead of your hiding in the kitchen, let's practice with you in the living room. What might you be doing there?

Keisha: Ironing. I always have ironing to do.

Trainer 2:   Good. Let's make this table be your ironing board and this book can be an iron. What else is in the living room?

Keisha: We've got a couch and a couple of chairs and a table and. . . .

Trainer 2:   How about if these three chairs become the couch and these can be the easy chairs. Is the door over here? Curt, why don't you come up here and stand at the door, ready to come in.

Trainer 1:   When your husband comes home in the afternoon, what's he likely to say to you if you're in the living room?

Keisha: Oh, something like, "Another day wasted; what's the use?" I used to try to cheer him up, but now I just hide.

Flo: He doesn't want to be cheered up.

Trainer 1:   That's a good point, Flo. Let's see if the steps for listening help Keisha find a better solution. The first step says to look at the person who's talking. So, when Curt, who is going to play the part of Kenny, comes through the door and starts complaining about his day, you're going to try to look at him. The next step says to think about what is being said. If you remember in the examples that we just showed you we "thought out loud" so that everyone could tell what we were thinking. That's what we'd like you to do. And then you do Step 3, "Wait your turn to speak." That's probably real important to do, since it sounds like Kenny has a lot on his mind.

Keisha: He may have a lot on his mind, but he doesn't have to take it out on me and the kids!

Trainer 2:   You're right, but maybe if you could let him know that you're listening and can understand how frustrating it gets, then he won't have to blow up at you.

Keisha: I hear what you're saying, but I don't know what to say to him when he's so upset.

Trainer 2:   Flo?

Flo: Just say, "It sounds like you had a rough day." He just needs a chance to let it out.

Keisha: Well, I'll try it, but I don't think it'll work.

Trainer 1:   That's why we're practicing it here, so that if doesn't go well, we can try something else. Curt, do you have a pretty good idea of what Kenny is like and what he might say?

Curt: Yeah, I think so. I'll come in mad and uptight and see how she handles it.

Trainer 1:   Exactly. You respond to what she does and says when you come home tired and frustrated. And the rest of the group will follow along with the steps as Debbie points them out up at the board. And I'll be right here, Keisha, in case you need any help. OK. Curt, it's late afternoon and you're coming through the front door.

Curt (as Kenny):   Where the hell is everybody? Oh, there you are. Where's the damn paper?

Trainer 1: Step 1 says to look at the person. Good. Now Step 2 is the one you usually think to yourself, but we'd like you to say it out loud.

Keisha: He's real upset again. He must have had another bad day. I'll wait until he's done.

Trainer 1: (whispers to Keisha) That was actually Steps 2 and 3. Now go on to Step 4.

Keisha: Sounds like you had a bad day.

Curt (as Kenny): Yeah, it was rough.

Trainer 1: OK. Let's stop there. Curt, as Kenny, how did Keisha do with her listening skills?

Curt: I think she did good. She was real calm and that helped a lot.

Trainer 1: Did you feel she was listening to you? What was helpful?

Curt: Yeah, I thought she was really listening because she stayed so calm and she didn't fuss and fidget around.

Trainer 1: That's real good feedback. Thanks, Curt, and thanks for playing the part of Kenny so well. Keisha, Curt felt that your being real still and calm helped him know that you were listening. Anything else?

Curt: Well, she stopped what she was doing and looked right at me.

Trainer 1: Good point. How about the rest of you? How do you think Keisha did? Did she do Step 1?

Flo: She was looking right at him.

Trainer 2: Good. Step 2. Frank?

Frank: She said she thought he was real upset.

Trainer 2: Thanks, Frank. That's right. That's the "think out loud" step. How about Step 3? Mary, did she wait her turn?

Mary: Yeah, she did.

Trainer 2: Good, Mary. I'm glad you were watching. Step 4 says to "say what you want to say." Did she do it? Arthur?

Arthur: She said he had a bad day.

Trainer 2: That's exactly right. And you were listening very well, too, Arthur. Any other comments or suggestions from the group? Anything that Keisha might do differently to make it even better?

Blanche: I think she talked very nice.

Trainer 1:   Thanks, Blanche. Both Debbie and I thought you did very well, too, Keisha. You waited, you didn't get upset, and you looked right at him. Those are all very important parts of listening. How do you think you did, Keisha?

Keisha: I guess I did OK. I was a little nervous at the beginning.

Trainer 1:   Sure, that's understandable. But you did it. Do you think you're ready to try it out in real life, with Kenny?

Keisha: I don't know. I guess so. But Kenny's not always as calm as Curt was.

Trainer 2:   I'm sure that's true. But Curt told you that your being calm helped him settle down. Maybe the same thing will work with Kenny. Let's fill out this Homework Report Form and then you can always decide later if you want to try the skill. OK?

Keisha: I guess so.

Trainer 2:   The first part asks for the name of the skill.

Keisha: Listening.

Trainer 2:   And the steps. You can copy them right from the board. And where will you try the skill?

Keisha: At home, with Kenny.

Trainer 2:   And when will you try it?

Keisha: I'm not sure I'm going to, but if I do, it'll be next Monday or Tuesday.

Trainer 2:   Good enough. We will all be eager to hear how it turned out.

Trainer 1:   That was a real good role play. Thank you, Keisha, and everyone. I think we still have time enough to go through another one. Does anyone have a situation in mind in which it would be helpful if they listened better?

Frank: Well, there's one I know I should work on, but I don't think I'm ready to try it out in real life.

Trainer 1:   This is a safe place to test it out. Can you tell us a little about it?

Frank: You know that my wife died almost a year ago. What with her being sick so long and then passing away, it's been real hard for me to get out of the house. Since she. . . died, I only go out when I have to, and to my doctor's appointments—he sent me to see the therapist—and now here. Well, I started to go back to church a few weeks ago, but it's hard. I don't really want to talk to anyone, so I come in late and sit at the back and then leave as soon as the service is over. Last week, my sister-in-law, Theresa, saw me, and I knew I should have waited outside after the service but I just wasn't up to it. But, one of these weeks, I'm gonna have to talk to her, I just know it.

Trainer 1: It sounds like an important step for you. Thank you for bringing it up. Would you like to work on it here?

Frank: I guess I better.

Trainer 1: Good. OK. Let's get some more information. You said that your sister-in-law, Theresa, is likely to approach you after church. Who here reminds you of your sister-in-law?

Frank: This lady, Flo. Same color hair.

Trainer 1: Good. Flo, would you help us out by taking the part of Theresa? Thanks. Come right up here. You said that she's apt to come up to you outside of church if you give her the chance. What's she likely to talk to you about?

Frank: Oh, you know, "We haven't seen you since the funeral and how are you getting along and the family is very concerned." And then she'll invite me for Sunday dinner. Don't get me wrong. They're nice people and all, but I'm not sure I'm ready.

Trainer 1: Let's give you some practice so at least you can feel more comfortable talking and listening, whenever you are ready. Flo, do you have an idea what Theresa is like and what she might say?

Flo: I think so.

Trainer 1: OK. Let's go through the steps. Step 1 tells you to look at the person who's talking. Step 2 reminds you to think about what's being said. What is Theresa (Flo) likely to say?

Frank: Just like I told you: "How have you been, we miss you, when will you come to dinner?"

Trainer 1: So, at Step 3, you wait your turn to talk and at Step 4, you say what you want to say.

Trainer 2: And we'd like the rest of you to pay close attention to how well Frank and Flo follow the steps for listening. Curt, would you watch for Step 1; Mary, Step 2; Arthur, 3; and Blanche, 4. OK. It's Sunday, after church, and Frank, where will you be?

Frank: Well, I think it would be better if I waited a couple of minutes for some of the other people to go out. I'm sure Theresa will catch me outside if I let her.

Trainer 2: So you'll just hold back a little, and Theresa will come up to you after you're outside. Flo, are you ready to approach Frank as he comes out of the church?

Flo: I guess so.

Trainer 2: Then let's begin. Jack will be at the board, pointing to the steps, and everyone else, pay close attention. Flo. . .

Flo (as Theresa): Frank, I'm glad I caught you. How have you been? The whole family's been worried about you. You must come to dinner.

Trainer 2: (whispers to Frank) Be sure to look at her and think about what she's saying. How are you going to respond?

Frank: Oh, hi, Theresa. I've been OK, thanks.

Flo (as Theresa): And how about dinner? Why don't you come today. We've got lots of food.

Frank: Thanks, Theresa, but could we make it next week?

Trainer 2: Very good. Let's stop right there and give Frank some feedback. Flo, how did he do? Do you think he was listening to you?

Flo: Well, he seemed a little uncomfortable, but he certainly was listening.

Trainer 2: Thanks, Flo, and thank you for being such a good Theresa. OK, let's go through the steps. Step 1, Curt?

Curt: Yeah, he was looking right at her.

Trainer 2: Thanks, Curt. Step 2, Mary? Did he think about what Theresa was saying?

Mary: I don't know.

Trainer 2: Remember that Step 2 is the "think out loud" step, and Frank didn't let us know what he was thinking. Step 3, Arthur, did he wait his turn to talk?

Arthur: He waited his turn to talk.

Trainer 2: Good, Arthur. And Blanche, Step 4.

Blanche: He said he'd go to dinner next week. That was a good idea.

Trainer 2:   Thanks, Blanche. Why do you think it was a good idea for him to say that he would go next week?

Blanche: Because he was probably too nervous to go that same day.

Trainer 2:   Good feedback, Blanche. Any other comments or suggestions for Frank?

Trainer 1:   Frank, I thought you did very well. And I agree with Blanche. Giving it a week might help you to get ready for the visit. And Flo, you did very well as Theresa.

Flo: Thanks. I know what it's like not to want to talk to people.

Trainer 2:   Well, you did an excellent job. And Frank, how do you feel you did?

Frank: I think I did OK, but I'm still not sure I'm ready to face the family.

Trainer 2:   We can certainly understand that. But, let's fill out a Homework Report Form anyway, and then you can decide when you'll actually try it out. It sounds like this is the situation you want to practice, it's just a question of when.

Frank: That's right.

Trainer 2:   OK. The top part of the form asks you what skill—listening—and the steps—up there on the board. Where? After church. With whom? Theresa. When? I guess that's still up in the air.

Frank: I don't know if I'm ready to try it this Sunday. But, if I do, I'll let you know.

Trainer 2:   That's great. Take it at your own pace. But you did very well in here.

Trainer 1:   You all did very well. But our time is about up for today. We'll meet in this same room at the same time next week. And, after we go through the homework reports from Keisha and maybe Frank, we'll try to give the rest of you a chance to practice the skill of listening. So, between now and then, be thinking about situations in which it would be helpful for you to be a better listener.

Second Session

In this session, trainers' goals include review of Structured Learning concepts and procedures, review of any homework from the previous session, and introduction and follow through on the skill to be taught that day. Although this sounds like a lot to cover, trainers will find that rapid pacing of sessions will allow them to cover a good deal of material, while also serving the purpose of keeping up trainee interest.

In reviewing homework assignments, it is extremely important to reinforce all early efforts. For those trainees who have not done their assignments, trainers will need to be sensitive to the possibility that leader expectations were unrealistic. Other possible reasons for uncompleted work might include insufficient rehearsal, no opportunity to try the skill, embarrassment, and so on. The possibility that trainees can complete their homework right in the group room should be considered (e.g., listening to another trainee about something he or she did during the week). This alternative, as a way of completing the homework, will give the trainee a success experience as well as ensuring the completion of the task.

Once discussion of homework has been completed, trainers should move on to discussion of the skill for that day. If the skill is the same as that from the previous session, care should be taken to provide additional modeling displays, with content different from that of the previous meeting. Role playing, feedback, and homework assignments follow.

Third and Later Sessions

The format just described should not vary much for later sessions. As trainees become more familiar with group procedures, leaders will be able to spend more time and attention on transfer of training and maintenance.

SUMMARY

This volume has introduced trainers to a method for teaching and enhancing social competency in a broad range of psychiatric clients. In offering a concrete training strategy as well as a specific menu of social skills, we have provided all of the tools necessary to start and follow through with a Structured Learning group. In this last chapter, we have fit the pieces together in a transcript of a basic Structured Learning group. The groups run by trainers in various settings may look rather different from the one depicted in this chapter. The principles in this volume can be implemented in many settings and at many levels of client sophistication,

References

Alberto, P. A., & Troutman, A. C. (1982). *Applied behavior analysis for teachers: Influencing student performance.* Columbus, OH: Charles E. Merrill.

American Journal of Insanity. (1847). *IV*(1).

Andrasik, F., & Matson, J. L. (1985). Social skills training for the mentally retarded. In L. L'Abate & M. A. Milan (Eds.), *Handbook of social skills training and research.* New York: Wiley.

Anthony, W. A., & Nemec, P. B. (1984). Psychiatric rehabilitation. In A. S. Bellack (Ed.), *Schizophrenia: Treatment, management, and rehabilitation.* New York: Grune & Stratton.

Arbuthnot, J. (1975). Modification of moral judgment through role playing. *Developmental Psychology, 11,* 319–324.

Atwater, S. K. (1953). Proactive inhibition and associative facilitation as affected by degree of prior learning. *Journal of Experimental Psychology, 46,* 400–404.

Ayllon, T., & Azrin, N. H. (1968). *The token economy: A motivational system for therapy and rehabilitation.* New York: Appleton-Century-Crofts.

Bandura, A. (1969). *Principles of behavior modification.* New York: Holt, Rinehart, & Winston.

Bandura, A., Blanchard, E. B., & Ritter, B. (1969). The relative efficacy of desensitization and modeling approaches for inducing behavioral, affective and attitudinal changes. *Journal of Personality and Social Psychology, 13,* 173–199.

Bandura, A., Ross, D., & Ross, S. A. (1961). Transmission of aggression through imitation of aggressive models. *Journal of Abnormal and Social Psychology, 63,* 575–582.

Becker, R. E., Heimberg, R. G., & Bellack, A. S. (1987). *Social skills training for depression.* New York: Pergamon.

Bellack, A. (1989). *A clinical guide for the treatment of schizophrenia.* New York: Plenum.

Borus, J. F. (1989). Chronic mental patients. In R. Michels (Ed.), *Psychiatry.* Philadelphia: Lippincott.

Brehm, J. W., & Cohen, A. R. (1962). *Explorations in cognitive dissonance.* New York: Wiley.

Bryan, J. H., & Test, M. A. (1967). Models and helping: Naturalistic studies in aiding behavior. *Journal of Personality and Social Psychology, 6,* 400–407.

Calabrese, D. N., & Hawkins, R. P. (1988). Job-related social skills training with female prisoners. *Behavior Modification, 12,* 3–34.

Callantine, M. F., & Warren, J. M. (1955). Learning sets in human concept formation. *Psychological Reports, 1,* 363–367.

Cantor, J. H. (1955). Amount of pretraining as a factor in stimulus predifferentiation and performance set. *Journal of Experimental Psychology, 50,* 180–184.

Chittenden, G. E. (1942). An experimental study in measuring and modifying assertive behavior in young children. *Monographs of the Society for Research in Child Development, 7(31).*

Clark, K. A., Christoff, K. A., & Hansen, D. J. (1986). Friendship-making training for psychiatric aftercare clients. *Journal of Partial Hospitalization, 3,* 273–284.

Cohen, A. R., & Latane, B. (1962). An experiment on choice in commitment to counter-attitudinal behavior. In J. W. Brehm & A. R. Cohen (Eds.), *Explorations in cognitive dissonance.* New York: Wiley.

Crafts, L. W. (1935). Transfer as related to number of common elements. *Journal of General Psychology, 13,* 147–158.

Culbertson, F. M. (1957). Modification of an emotionally held attitude through role playing. *Journal of Abnormal and Social Psychology, 54,* 230–233.

Davis, K., & Jones, E. E. (1960). Changes in interpersonal perception as a means of reducing cognitive dissonance. *Journal of Abnormal and Social Psychology, 61,* 402–410.

Deguchi, H. (1984). Observational learning from a radical-behaviorist viewpoint. *The Behavior Analyst, 7,* 83–95.

Diamond, R. (1985). Drugs and the quality of life: The patient's point of view. *Journal of Clinical Psychiatry, 46,* 29–35.

Donahoe, C. P., & Driesenga, S. A. (1988). A review of social skills training with chronic mental patients. In M. Hersen, R. M. Eisler, & P. M. Miller (Eds.), *Progress in behavior modification (Vol. 23).* Beverly Hills, CA: Sage.

Dreikers, R., Schulman, B. H., & Mosak, H. (1952). Patient-therapist in multiple psychotherapy: Its advantages to the therapist. *Psychiatric Quarterly, 26,* 219–227.

Duncan, C. P. (1953). Transfer in motor learning as a function of degree of first-task learning and inner-task similarity. *Journal of Experimental Psychology, 45,* 1–11.

Duncan, C. P. (1958). Transfer after training with single versus multiple tasks. *Journal of Experimental Psychology, 55,* 63–73.

Ellis, H. (1965). *The transfer of learning.* New York: Macmillan.

Epps, S., Thompson, B. J., & Lane, M. P. (1985). *Procedures for incorporating generalization programming into interventions for behaviorally disordered students.* Unpublished manuscript, Iowa State University, Ames.

Erickson, R., & Burton, M. (1986). Working with psychiatric patients with cognitive deficits. *Cognitive Rehabilitation,* July/August, 26–31.

Feshback, S. (1964). The function of aggression and the regulation of aggressive drive. *Psychological Review, 71,* 247–272.

Feindler, E. L., & Ecton, R. B. (1986). *Adolescent anger control: Cognitive-behavioral techniques.* New York: Pergamon.

Frank, J. D. (1973). *Persuasion and healing.* New York: Schocken Books.

Friedenberg, W. P. (1971). *Verbal and non-verbal attraction modeling in an initial interview analogue.* Unpublished masters thesis, Syracuse University.

Gagne, R. M., Baker, K. E. & Foster, H. (1950). On the relation between similarity and transfer of training in the learning of discriminative motor tasks. *Psychological Review, 57,* 67–79.

Gagne, R. M., & Foster, H. (1949). Transfer to a motor skill from practice on a pictured representation. *Journal of Experimental Psychology, 39,* 342–354.

Galassi, J. P., & Galassi, M. D. (1984). Promoting transfer and maintenance of counseling outcomes. In S. D. Brown & R. W. Lent (Eds.), *Handbook of counseling psychology.* New York: Wiley.

Gambrill, E. D. (1983). Behavioral intervention with child abuse and neglect. In M. Hersen, R. M. Eisler, & P. M. Miller (Eds.), *Progress in behavior modification (Vol. 15).* New York: Academic.

Gelfand, D. M., & Singer, R. D. (1968). Generalization of reinforced personality evaluations: A further investigation. *Journal of Clinical Psychology, 24*, 24–26.

Goldbeck, R. A., Bernstein, B. B., Hellix, W. A., & Marx, M. H. (1957). Application of the half-split technique to problem-solving tasks. *Journal of Experimental Psychology, 53*, 330–338.

Goldstein, A. P. (1971) *Psychotherapeutic attraction*. New York: Pergamon Press.

Goldstein, A. P., Heller, K., & Sechrest, L. B. (1966). *Psychotherapy and the psychology of behavior change*. New York: Wiley.

Goldstein, A. P. (1973). *Structured Learning therapy: Toward a psychotherapy for the poor*. New York: Academic.

Goldstein, A. P., Sprafkin, R. P., & Gershaw, N. J. (1976). *Skill training for community living*. New York: Pergamon.

Goldstein, A. P., Sprafkin, R. P., Gershaw, N. J., & Klein, P. (1980). *Skillstreaming the adolescent*. Champaign, IL: Research Press.

Haley, J. (1976). *Problem solving therapy*. San Francisco: Jossey-Bass.

Hall, S. M., Loeb, P., Coyne, K., & Cooper, J. (1981). Increasing employment in ex-heroin addicts I: Criminal justice sample. *Behavior Therapy, 12*, 443–452.

Harvey, O. J., & Beverly, G. D. (1961). Some personality correlates of concept change through role playing. *Journal of Abnormal and Social Psychology, 63*, 125–130.

Hayward, M. L., Peters, J. J., & Taylor, J. E. (1952). Some values of the use of multiple therapists in treatment of psychoses. *Psychiatric Quarterly, 26*, 244–249.

Hendrickson, G., & Schroeder, W. H. (1941). Transfer of training in learning to hit a submerged target. *Journal of Educational Psychology, 32*, 205–213.

Hierholzer, R. W., & Liberman, R. P. (1986). Successful living: A social skills and problem-solving group for the chronic mentally ill. *Hospital and Community Psychiatry, 37*, 913–918.

Hildum, D. C., & Brown, R. W. (1956). Verbal reinforcement and interviewer bias. *Journal of Abnormal and Social Psychology, 53*, 108–111.

Hollander, T. G. (1970). *The effects of role playing on attraction, disclosure, and attitude change in a psychotherapy analogue*. Unpublished doctoral dissertation, Syracuse University.

Hollin, C. R., & Trower, P. (1988). Development and applications of social skill training: A review and critique. In M. Hersen, R. M. Eiser, & P. M. Miller (Eds.), *Progress in behavior modification (Vol. 22)*. Newbury Park, CA: Sage.

Holmes, D. S. (1971). Round robin therapy: A technique for implementing the effects of psychotherapy. *Journal of Consulting and Clinical Psychology, 37*, 324–331.

Iannotti, R. J. (1977). Effect of role-taking experiences on role taking, empathy, altruism, and aggression. *Developmental Psychology, 13*, 274–281.

Jamison, R. N., Lambert, E. W., & McCloud, D. J. (1985). Social skills training with hospitalized adolescents: An evaluative experiment. *Adolescence, 21*, 55–65.

Janis, I. L., & Mann, L. (1965). Effectiveness of emotional role playing in modifying smoking habits and attitudes. *Journal of Experimental Research in Personality, 1*, 84–90.

Kanfer, F. H., & Karoly, P. (1972). Self-control: A behavioristic excursion into the lion's den. *Behavior therapy, 3*, 398–416.

Kaplan, H. I., & Sadock, B. J. (Eds.). (1989). *Comprehensive textbook of psychiatry, (Vol. V)*. Baltimore: Williams & Wilkins.

Karasu, T. B. (1989) (Eds.). *Treatment of psychiatric disorders*. Washington, D. C.: American Psychiatric Association.

Karoly, P., & Steffen, J. J. (Eds.). (1980). *Improving the long term effects of psychotherapy*. New York: Gardner.

Kazdin, A. E. (1975). *Behavior modification in applied settings*. Homewood, IL: Dorsey.

Kelly, G. A. (1955). *The psychology of personal constructs*. New York: Norton.

Kendall, P. C. & Braswell, L. (1982). Cognitive-behavioral self-control therapy for children: a component analysis. *Journal of Consulting and Clinical Psychology, 50*, 672–689.

Kendall, P. C., & Braswell, L. (1985). *Cognitive-behavioral therapy for impulsive children*. New York: Guilford.

Kleinsasser, L. D. (1968). *The reduction of performance anxiety as a function of desensitization, pre-therapy vicarious learning, and vicarious learning alone*. Unpublished doctoral dissertation, Pennsylvania State University.

Klinger, B. I. (1970). Effect of peer model responsiveness and length of induction procedure on hypnotic responsiveness. *Journal of Abnormal Psychology, 75*, 15–18.

Krumboltz, J. D., & Thoresen, C. E. (1964). The effects of behavioral counseling in group and individual settings on information seeking behavior. *Journal of Counseling Psychology, 11*, 324–333.

Krumboltz, J. D., Varenhorst, B. B., & Thoresen, C. E. (1967). Non-verbal factors in the effectiveness of models in counseling. *Journal of Counseling Psychology, 14*, 412–418.

Lefkowitz, M., Blake, R. R., & Mouton, J. S. (1954). Status factors in pedestrian violation of traffic signals. *Journal of Abnormal and Social Psychology, 51*, 704–706.

Levine, J., & Zigler, E. (1973). The essential-reactive distinction in alcoholism. *Journal of Abnormal Psychology, 81*, 242–249.

Lewinsohn, P. M. (1975). The behavioral study and treatment of depression. In M. Hersen, R. Eisler, & P. Miller (Eds.), *Progress in behavior modification (Vol. 1)*. New York: Academic.

Liberman, B. (1970). *The effects of modeling procedures on attraction and disclosure in a psychotherapy analogue*. Unpublished doctoral dissertation, Syracuse University.

Liberman, R. P., Falloon, I. R. H., & Aitchison, R. A. (1984). Multiple family therapy for schizophrenics: A behavioral approach. *Psychosocial Rehabilitation Journal, 4*, 60–77.

Liberman, R. P., & Foy, D. W. (1983). Psychiatric rehabilitation for chronic mental patients. *Psychiatric Annals, 13*, 539–545.

Liberman, R. P., King, L. W., & DeRisi, W. J. (1975). *Personal effectiveness: Guiding people to assert themselves and improve their social skills*. Champaign, IL: Research Press.

Lichtenstein, E., Keutzer, C. S., & Himes, K. H. (1969). Emotional role playing and changes in smoking attitudes and behaviors. *Psychological Reports, 23*, 379–387.

MacGregor, R., Ritchie, A. M., Serrano, A. C., & Schuster, F. P. (1964). *Multiple impact theory with families*. New York: McGraw-Hill.

Mandler, G. (1954). Transfer of training as a function of degree of response overlearning. *Journal of Experimental Psychology, 47*, 411–417.

Mandler, G., & Heinemann, S. H. (1956). Effect of overlearning of a verbal response on transfer of training. *Journal of Experimental Psychology, 52*, 39–46.

Mann, J. H. (1956). Experimental evaluations of role playing. *Psychological Bulletin, 53*, 227–234.

Marlatt, G. A., & Gordon, J. A. (1980). Determinants of relapse: Implications for the maintenance of behavior change. In P. O. Davidson & S. M. Davidson (Eds.), *Behavioral medicine: Changing health lifestyles*. New York: Brunner/Mazel.

Marlatt, G. A., Jacobson, E. A., Johnson, D. L., & Morrice, D. J. (1970). Effect of exposure to a model receiving evaluative feedback upon subsequent behavior in an interview. *Journal of Consulting and Clinical Psychology, 34*, 194–212.

Mastria, E. O., Mastria, M. A., & Harkins, J. C. (1979). Treatment of child abuse by behavioral intervention: a case report. *Child Welfare, 58*, 253–261.

Matarazzo, J. D., Wiens, A. N., & Saslow, G. (1965). Studies in interview speech behavior. In L. Krasner & L. P. Ullman (Eds.), *Research in behavior modification*. New York: Holt, Rinehart & Winston.

McFall, R. M., & Marston, A. R. (1970). An experimental investigation of behavior rehearsal in assertive training. *Journal of Abnormal Psychology, 76*, 295–303.

McGehee, N., & Thayer, P. W. (1961). *Training in business and industry*. New York: Wiley.

McGinnis, E., & Goldstein, A. P. (1984). *Skillstreaming the elementary school child: A guide for teaching prosocial skills*. Champaign, IL: Research Press.

Milan, M. A., (1987). Behavioral procedures in closed institutions. In E. K. Morris & C. J. Bauckmann (Eds.). *Behavioral approaches to crime and delinquency*. New York: Plenum Press.

Milby, J. B. (1970). Modification of extreme social isolation by contingent social reinforcement. *Journal of Applied Behavior Analysis, 3,* 149–152.

Mueser, K. T., & Liberman, R. P. (1988). Vocational skills training. In J. A. Ciardello & M. D. Bell (Eds.), *Vocational rehabilitation of persons with prolonged mental illness*. Baltimore: Johns Hopkins University Press.

Mueser, K. T., Valenti-Hein, D., & Yarnold, P. R. (1987). Dating skills groups for the developmentally disabled. *Behavior Modification, 11,* 200–228.

Nay, W. R. (1979). Parents as real-life reinforcers: The enhancement of parent-training effects across conditions other than training. In A. P. Goldstein & F. H. Kanfer (Eds.), *Maximizing treatment gains*. New York: Academic.

Neiland, T. H. & Israel, A. D. (1981). Toward Maintenance and generalization of behavior change; Teaching children self-regulation and self-instructional skills. *Cognitive Therapy and Research, 5,* 189–195

Nuechterlein, K. H., & Dawson, M. E. (1984). A heuristic vulnerability/stress model of schizophrenic episodes. *Schizophrenia Bulletin, 10,* 300–312.

Nuthman, A. M. (1957). Conditioning a response class on a personality test. *Journal of Abnormal and Social Psychology, 54,* 19–23.

O'Leary, D. E., O'Leary, M. R., & Donovan, D. M. (1976). Social skill acquisition and psychological development of alcoholics: a review. *Addictive Behaviors, 1,* 111–120.

Osgood, C. E. (1949). The similarity paradox in human learning: A resolution. *Psychological Review, 56,* 132–143.

Osgood, C. E. (1953). *Method and theory in experimental psychology*. New York: Oxford.

Patterson, G. R., & Brodsky, G. A. (1966). A behavior modification program for a child with multiple problem behaviors. *Journal of Child Psychiatry, 7,* 277–295.

Perry, M. A. (1970). *Didactic instruction for and modeling of empathy*. Unpublished doctoral dissertation, Syracuse University.

Phillips, E. L. (1956). *Psychotherapy: A modern theory and practice*. Englewood Cliffs, NJ: Prentice-Hall.

Plienis, A. J., Hansen, D. J., Ford, F., Smith, S. Jr., Stark, L. J., & Kelly, J. A. (1987). Behavioral small group training to improve the social skills of emotionally disordered adolescents. *Behavior Therapy, 18,* 17–32.

Quay, H. (1959). The effect of verbal reinforcement on the recall of early memories. *Journal of Abnormal and Social Psychology, 59,* 254–257.

Radke-Yarrow, M., Zahn-Waxler, C., & Chapman, M. (1983). Children's prosocial dispositions and behavior. In P. H. Musser (Ed.). *Handbook of child psychology*. New York: Wiley.

Rathjen, D., Hiniker, A., & Rathjen, E. (1976). *Incorporation of behavioral techniques in a game format to teach children social skills*. Paper presented at the meeting of the Association for Advancement of Behavior Therapy, New York.

Ritter, B. (1969). Treatment of acrophobia with contact desensitization. *Behavior Research and Therapy, 7,* 41–45.

Rogers, C. R. (1951). *Client centered therapy*. Cambridge, MA: Houghton-Mifflin.

Ross, D. M., Ross, S. A., & Evans, T. A. (1976). The modification of extreme social withdrawal by modeling with guided participation. *Journal of Behavior Therapy and Experimental Psychiatry, 2,* 273–279.

Salter, A. (1949). *Conditioned reflex therapy.* New York: Creative Age Press.

Salzinger, K., & Pisoni, S. (1957). Reinforcement of verbal affect responses of schizophrenics during the clinical interview. Paper presented at the American Psychological Association, New York.

Schnelle, J. F., Geller, E. S., & Davis, M. A. (1987). Law enforcement and crime prevention. In E. S. Morris & C. J. Braukmann (Eds.). *Behavioral approaches to crime and delinquency.* New York: Plenum Press.

Schofield, W. (1964). *Psychotherapy: The purchase of friendship.* Englewood Cliffs, NJ: Prentice-Hall.

Sherman, A. R. (1979). In vivo therapies for phobic reactions, instrumental behavior problems, and interpersonal communication problems. In A. P. Goldstein & F. H. Kanfer (Eds.), *Maximizing treatment gains.* New York: Academic.

Sherman, A. R., & Levine, M. P. (1979). In vivo therapies for compulsive habits, sexual difficulties, and severe adjustment problems. In A. P. Goldstein & F. H. Kanfer (Eds.), *Maximizing treatment gains.* New York: Academic.

Shore, E., & Sechrest, L. (1961). Concept attainment as a function of number of positive instances presented. *Journal of Educational Psychology, 52,* 303–307.

Slavin, D. R. (1967). *Response transfer of conditional affective responses as a function of an experimental analog of psychotherapy.* Unpublished doctoral dissertation, Northwestern University.

Spivack, G., & Shure, M. (1974). *Social adjustment of young children.* San Francisco: Jossey-Bass.

Sprafkin, R. P. (1984). Social skills training. In R. J. Corsini (Ed.), *Encyclopedia of psychology.* New York: Wiley.

Staub, E. (1971). The learning and unlearning of aggression. In J. Singer (Ed.), *The control of aggression and violence.* New York: Academic.

Steiner, C., Wyckoff, H., Marcus, J., Lariviere, P., Goldstine, D., & Schwebel, R. (1975). *Readings in radical psychiatry.* New York: Grove.

Stokes, T. F., & Baer, D. M. (1977). An implicit technology of generalization. *Journal of Applied Behavior Analysis, 10,* 349–367.

Stravynski, A., Grey, S., & Elie, R. (1987). Outline of the therapeutic process in social skills training and socially dysfunctional patients. *Journal of Consulting and Clinical Psychology, 55,* 224–228.

Sulzer-Azaroff, B., & Mayer, G. R. (1977). *Applying behavior analysis procedures with children and youth.* New York: Holt, Rinehart & Winston.

Sutton, K. (1970). *Effects of modeled empathy and structured social class upon level of therapist displayed empathy.* Unpublished doctoral dissertation, Syracuse University.

Tharp, R. G., & Wetzel, R. J. (1969). *Behavior modification in the natural environment.* New York: Academic.

Thorndike, E. L., & Woodworth, R. S. (1901). The influence of improvement in one mental function upon the efficiency of other functions. *Psychological Review, 6,* 247–261.

Turner, S. M., Hersen, M., & Bellack, A. S. (1978). Use of social skills training to teach prosocial behaviors in an organically impaired and retarded patient. *Journal of Behavior Therapy and Experimental Psychiatry, 9,* 253–358.

Ulmer, G. (1939). Teaching geometry to cultivate reflective thinking: An experimental study with 1239 high school students. *Journal of Experimental Education, 8,* 18–25.

Underwood, B. J. (1951). Associative transfer in verbal learning as a function of response similarity and degree of first-list learning. *Journal of Experimental Psychology, 42,* 44–53.

Underwood, B. J., & Schultz, R. W. (1960). *Meaningfulness and verbal behavior*. New York: Lippincott.

Verplanck, W. S. (1955). The control of the content of conversation: Reinforcements of statements of opinion. *Journal of Abnormal and Social Psychology, 51*, 668–676.

Walker, H. M., Hops, H., & Johnson, S. M. (1975). Generalization and maintenance of classroom treatment effects. *Behavior Therapy, 6*, 188–200.

Walsh, W. (1971). *The effects of conformity pressure and modeling on the attraction of hospitalized patients toward an interviewer*. Unpublished doctoral dissertation, Syracuse University.

Whitaker, C. A., Malone, T. P., & Warkentin, J. (1966). Multiple therapy and psychotherapy. In F. Fromm-Reichmann & M. Morens (Eds.), *Progress in psychotherapy*. New York: Grune & Stratton.

Wildman, B. G., Wildman, H. E., & Kelly, J. W. (1986). Group conversational skills training and social validation with mentally retarded adults. *Applied Research in Mental Retardation, 7*, 443–458.

Wolpe, J. (1958). *Psychotherapy by reciprocal inhibition*. Stanford, CA: Stanford University Press.

Wolpe, J., & Lazarus, A. A. (1966). *Behavior therapy techniques*. New York: Pergamon.

Young, R. K., & Underwood, B. J. (1954). Transfer in verbal materials with dissimilar stimuli and response similarity varied. *Journal of Experimental Psychology, 47*, 153–159.

Zubin, J., & Spring, B (1977). Vulnerability: A new view of schizophrenia. *Journal of Abnormal Psychology, 86*, 103–126.

Appendix

Name _____ Date _____

Listed below you will find a number of skills that your client is more or less proficient in using. This checklist will help you to evaluate your individual client's proficiency in each skill. This information can then be used in grouping trainees into Structured Learning groups. It can also be used in deciding which skills to teach once groups have been formed.

Circle 1 if the client is never good at using the skill.
Circle 2 if the client is seldom good at using the skill.
Circle 3 if the client is sometimes good at using the skill.
Circle 4 if the client is usually good at using the skill.
Circle 5 if the client is always good at using the skill.

Beginning Social Skills

1   2   3   4   5   1. Starting a conversation: Is your client comfortable initiating conversations, choosing an appropriate time and place, beginning with light topics and leading into more serious topics?

1   2   3   4   5   2. Listening: Does your client pay attention when someone else is talking and make an effort to understand what is being said?

1   2   3   4   5   3. Ending a conversation: Is your client comfortable ending conversations, making appropriate closing remarks?

1   2   3   4   5   4. Asking for help: Does your client appropriately request assistance when he or she is having difficulty?

Continued

127

Structured Learning Skill Questionnaire.

Beginning Social Skills. *Continued*

1   2   3   4   5   5. Following instructions: Does your client pay attention to instructions and carry them out appropriately?

1   2   3   4   5   6. Giving a compliment: Is your client comfortable telling others he or she likes something about them or their activities?

1   2   3   4   5   7. Saying "thank you": Does your client let others know he or she appreciates things they have done?

1   2   3   4   5   8. Apologizing: Does your client tell others he or she is sorry after doing something wrong?

Skills for Dealing with Feelings

1   2   3   4   5   9. Expressing your feelings: Is your client aware of his or her feelings? Does he or she express feelings in socially acceptable ways?

1   2   3   4   5   10. Understanding the feelings of others: Does your client understand and express an appreciation of the feelings of others?

1   2   3   4   5   11. Preparing for a stressful conversation: Does your client plan the best way to present his or her point of view prior to a stressful conversation?

1   2   3   4   5   12. Reacting to failure: Does your client figure out the reason for failing in a particular situation and what he or she can do about it in order to be more successful in the future?

Assertiveness Skills

1   2   3   4   5   13. Standing up for your rights: Does your client assert his or her rights by letting others know where he or she stands on an issue?

1   2   3   4   5   14. Helping others: Does your client offer help to others who may need or want it?

1   2   3   4   5   15. Giving instructions: Does your client explain to others how they are to do a specific task?

1   2   3   4   5   16. Making a complaint: Does your client tell others when they are responsible for creating a particular problem for him or her?

Continued

Assertiveness Skills. *Continued*

1	2	3	4	5	17.	Answering a complaint: Does your client work toward arriving at a fair solution to someone else's complaint?
1	2	3	4	5	18.	Negotiation: Does your client arrive at a plan that satisfies him- or herself and others who have taken different positions on the issue at hand?
1	2	3	4	5	19.	Self-control: Does your client control his or her temper so that things do not get out of hand?
1	2	3	4	5	20.	Persuasion: Does your client use persuasion by expressing his or her position while considering the feelings and ideas of the other person?
1	2	3	4	5	21.	Responding to persuasion: Does your client carefully consider another person's position, compare it with his or her own, before deciding what to do?
1	2	3	4	5	22.	Dealing with group pressure: Does your client decide for him or herself what to do when others pressure him or her to do something?

Problem-solving Skills

1	2	3	4	5	23.	Setting priorities: Does your client decide which of a number of problems is most important and should be dealt with first?
1	2	3	4	5	24.	Making decisions: Does your client consider alternatives and make decisions in his or her best interest?
1	2	3	4	5	25.	Setting a goal: Does your client realistically decide what he or she can accomplish before beginning a task?
1	2	3	4	5	26.	Concentrating on a task: Does your client make those preparations which will help get a job done?
1	2	3	4	5	27.	Rewarding yourself: Does your client decide whether a task which he or she has accomplished deserves a reward, and provide appropriate self-rewards?

Author Index

Subject Index

Psychology Practitioner Guidebooks

Stress Inoculation Training
Donald Meichenbaum
ISBN: 0–205–14418–7

Management of Chronic Headaches:
A Psychological Approach
Edward D. Blanchard & Fran Andrasik
ISBN: 0–205–14284–2

Clinical Utilization of Microcomputer Technology
Raymond G. Romanczyk
ISBN: 0–205–14468–3

Marital Therapy: A Behavioral-
Communications Approach
Philip H. Bornstein & Marcy T. Bornstein
ISBN: 0–205–14289–3

Psychological Consultation in the Courtroom
Michael T. Nietzel & Ronald C. Dillehay
ISBN: 0–205–14426–8

Group Cognitive Therapy: A Treatment Approach for
Depressed Older Adults
Elizabeth E. Yost, Larry E. Beutler, M. Anne Corbishley
& James R. Allender
ISBN: 0–205–14516–7

Dream Analysis in Psychotherapy
Lillie Weiss
ISBN: 0–205–14499–3

Understanding and Treating Attention
Deficient Disorder
Edward A. Kirby & Liam K. Grimley
ISBN: 0–205–14391–1

Language and Speech Disorders in Children
Jon Eisenson
ISBN: 0–205–14315–6

Adolescent Anger Control: Cognitive-Behavioral Techniques
Eva L. Feindler & Randolph B. Ecton
ISBN: 0–205–14324–5

**Pediatric Psychology: Psychological Interventions and
Strategies for Pediatric Problems**
Michael C. Roberts
ISBN: 0–205–14465–9

Treating Childhood and Adolescent Obesity
Daniel S. Kirschenbaum, William G. Johnson &
Peter M. Stalonas, Jr.
ISBN: 0–205–14393–8

**Eating Disorders: Management of Obesity, Bulimia
and Anorexia Nervosa**
W. Stewart Agras
ISBN: 0–205–14262–1

**Treatment of Depression:
An Interpersonal Systems Approach**
Ian H. Gotlib & Catherine A. Colby
ISBN: 0–205–14357–1

Psychology as a Profession: Foundations of Practice
Walter B. Pryzwansky & Robert N. Wendt
ISBN: 0–205–14459–4

Multimethod Assessment of Chronic Pain
Paul Karoly & Mark P. Jensen
ISBN: 0–205–14385–7

Hypnotherapy: A Modern Approach
William L. Golden, E. Thomas Dowd & Fred Friedberg
ISBN: 0–205–14334–2

Behavioral Treatment for Persistent Insomnia
Patricia Lacks
ISBN: 0–205–14399–7

The Physically and Sexually Abused Child:
Evaluation and Treatment
C. Eugene Walker, Barbara L. Bonner & Keith L. Kaufman
ISBN: 0–205–14493–4

Social Skills Training Treatment for Depression
Robert E. Becker, Richard G. Heimberg & Alan S. Bellack
ISBN: 0–205–14273–7

Teaching Child Management Skills
Richard F. Dangel & Richard A. Polster
ISBN: 0–205–14308–3

Rational-Emotive Therapy with Alcoholics and
Substance Abusers
Albert Ellis, John F. McInerney, Raymond DiGiuseppe &
Raymond J. Yeager
ISBN: 0–205–14320–2

Non-Drug Treatments for Essential Hypertension
Edward B. Blanchard, John E. Martin
& Patricia M. Dubbert
ISBN: 0–205–14286–9

Treating Obsessive-Compulsive Disorder
Samuel M. Turner & Deborah C. Beidel
ISBN: 0–205–14488–8

Self-Esteem Enhancement with Children
and Adolescents
Alice W. Pope, Susan M. McHale &
W. Edward Craighead
ISBN: 0–205–14455–1

Preventing Substance Abuse Among
Children and Adolescents
Jean E. Rhodes & Leonard A. Jason
ISBN: 0–205–14463–2

Clinical Practice in Adoption
Robin C. Winkler, Dirck W. Brown,
Margaret van Keppel & Amy Blanchard
ISBN: 0–205–14512–4

Behavioral Relaxation Training and Assessment
Roger Poppen
ISBN: 0–205–14457–8

Adult Obesity Therapy
Michael D. LeBow
ISBN: 0–205–14404–7

Social Skills Training for Psychiatric Patients
Robert Paul Liberman, William J. DeRisi & Kim T. Mueser
ISBN: 0–205–14406–3

Treating Depression in Children and Adolescents
Johnny L. Matson
ISBN: 0–205–14414–4

The Practice of Brief Psychotherapy
Sol L. Garfield
ISBN: 0–205–14329–6

Reducing Delinquency:
Intervention in the Community
Arnold P. Goldstein, Barry Glick, Mary Jane Irwin, Claudia
Pask-McCartney & Ibrahim Rubama
ISBN: 0–205–14338–5

Rational-Emotive Couples Therapy
Albert Ellis, Joyce L. Sichel, Raymond J. Yeager,
Dominic J. DiMattia, & Raymond DiGiuseppe
ISBN: 0–205–14317–2 Paper   0–205–14433–0 Cloth

Cognitive-Behavioral Interventions with Young Offenders
Clive R. Hollin
ISBN: 0–205–14368–7 Paper   0–205–14369–5 Cloth

Gestalt Therapy: Practice and Theory, Second Edition
Margaret P. Korb, Jeffrey Gorrell & Vernon Van De Riet
ISBN: 0–205–14395–4 Paper   0–205–14396–2 Cloth

Assessment of Eating Disorders: Obesity, Anorexia
and Bulimia Nervosa
Donald A. Williamson
ISBN: 0–205–14507–8 Paper   0–205–14508–6 Cloth

Body Image Disturbance: Assessment and Treatment
J. Kevin Thompson
ISBN: 0–205–14482–9 Paper   0–205–14483–7 Cloth

Suicide Risk: Assessment and Response Guidelines
William J. Fremouw, Maria de Perczel & Thomas E. Ellis
ISBN: 0–205–14327–X Paper   0–205–14328–8 Cloth

**Treating Conduct and Oppositional Defiant
Disorders in Children**
Arthur M. Horne & Thomas V. Sayger
ISBN: 0–205–14371–7 Paper   0–205–14372–5 Cloth

Counseling the Bereaved
Richard A. Dershimer
ISBN: 0–205–14310–5 Paper   0–205–14311–3 Cloth

Behavioral Medicine: Concepts and Procedures
Eldon Tunks & Anthony Bellissimo
ISBN: 0–205–14484–5 Paper   0–205–14485–3 Cloth

Drug Therapy for Behavior Disorders: An Introduction
Alan Poling, Kenneth D. Gadow & James Cleary
ISBN: 0–205–14453–5 Paper   0–205–14454–3 Cloth

**The Personality Disorders:
A Psychological Approach to Clinical Management**
Ira Daniel Turkat
ISBN: 0–205–14486–1 Paper   0–205–14487–X Cloth

**Treatment of Rape Victims:
Facilitating Psychosocial Adjustment**
Karen S. Calhoun & Beverly M. Atkeson
ISBN: 0–205–14296–6 Paper   0–205–14297–4 Cloth

**Psychotherapy and Counseling with Minorities:
A Cognitive Approach to Individual and Cultural Differences**
Manuel Ramirez III
ISBN: 0–205–14461–6

Coping with Ethical Dilemmas in Psychotherapy
Martin Lakin
ISBN: 0–205–14401–2 Paper   0–205–14402–0 Cloth

Anxiety Disorders: A Rational-Emotive Perspective
Ricks Warren & George D. Zgourides
ISBN: 0–205–14497–7 Paper   0–205–14498–5 Cloth

Preventing Relapse in the Addictions:
A Biopsychosocial Approach
Emil J. Chiauzzi
ISBN: 0–205–14303–2 Paper   0–205–14304–0 Cloth

Behavioral Family Intervention
Matthew R. Sanders & Mark R. Dadds
ISBN: 0–205–14599–X Paper   0–205–14600–7 Cloth

Anxiety Disorders in Youth:
Cognitive-Behavioral Interventions
Philip C. Kendall
ISBN: 0–205–14589–2 Paper   0–205–14590–6 Cloth

Psychological Treatment of Cancer Patients:
A Cognitive-Behavioral Approach
William L. Golden, Wayne D. Gersh & David M. Robbins
ISBN: 0–205–14551–5 Paper   0–205–14552–3 Cloth

School Consultation: Practice and Training,
Second Edition
Jane Close Conoley & Collie W. Conoley
ISBN: 0–205–14561–2 Paper   0–205–14564–7 Cloth

Posttraumatic Stress Disorder: A Behavioral Approach
to Assessment and Treatment
Philip A. Saigh
ISBN: 0–205–14553–1 Paper   0–205–14554–X Cloth

Cognitive Therapy of Borderline Personality Disorder
Mary Anne Layden, Cory F. Newman, Arthur Freeman
& Susan Byers Morse
ISBN: 0–205–14808–5 Paper   0–205–14807–7 Cloth

Social Skills for Mental Health:
A Structured Learning Approach
Robert P. Sprafkin, N. Jane Gershaw & Arnold P. Goldstein
ISBN: 0–205–14842–5 Paper   0–205–14841–7 Cloth

**Managed Mental Health Care: A Guide for Practitioners,
Employers, and Hospital Administrators**
Thomas R. Giles
ISBN: 0–205–14839–5 Paper   0–205–14838–7 Cloth